THEY WERE
BOTH NAKED,
THE MAN,
AND HIS WIFE

The secret of sexual intimacy in marriage

PROF. MICHAEL T. ADENITIRE FABI; PH.D

Paperback: 978-1-969919-35-0
eBook: 978-1-969919-36-7
Library of Congress Control Number: 2025922500

This is a work of nonfiction.

Ordering Information:

Prime Seven Media
518 Landmann St.
Tomah City, WI 54660

Printed in the United States of America

TABLE OF CONTENTS

AKNOWLEDGEMENTS

My profound gratitude goes to the Almighty GOD:
the FATHER, the SON, and the HOLY SPIRIT,
for His grace to put this book together.

I acknowledge the students at Zoe Pentecostal
Bible Institute & Seminary, both past and present,
for your contribution in the classroom as we
studied together some sections of the book.

I acknowledge all the members of Zoe Pentecostal Mission,
where I have preached most of the messages in this book.

I cannot forget my wife, Dr. Mabel Olufunmilayo Adenitire,
who created the enabling environment for this book.

To my late Mother, Madam Victoria Adenitire, though
you have gone to rest with the LORD, your investment
in my education has made this book possible.

DEDICATION

I dedicate this book to those couples who have upheld
biblical values in their marriage and have given room to
enjoy intimacy in their marriage despite many challenges.

INTRODUCTION

My amazing reader!

Welcome to this wild ride, my friends! You've just cracked open the book that's going to take you on a rollercoaster of thoughts, emotions, and revelations. This book, born out of countless sleepless nights filled with caffeine and inspiration, is a culmination of years of passionate exploration. The idea struck me like lightning one quiet evening; I realized there were so many untold stories waiting to burst forth. I wanted to create something that resonates with human experience and pulls at those heartstrings. It's not just a book; it's a conversation, a companion for your thoughts and musing.

As I delved into the research, I found myself immersed in a vast array of ideas and histories. I ventured through libraries, scoured old archives, and absorbed every fragment that could add depth to my narrative. Each chapter has layers and textures that weave together the beautifully chaotic tapestry of life. I wanted this book to be alive, spirited, and bold, much like the people it is intended for. The quest was not just about gathering facts; it was about finding the soul behind every story.

You might wonder, why should you care? Why should you stick with me until the last page? Well, dear reader, let me assure you, this journey isn't just about facts and figures. It's about feelings, triumphs, and those gritty moments that redefine who we are. I firmly believe that every page you turn will take you deeper into a realm that is not just educational but transformative. I promise you laughter, tears, and maybe a few "aha!" moments that'll leave you pondering long after you set the book down.

Writing this book has felt like raising a child. I nurtured it with love and sweat, and now I'm sending it into the world, hoping it will inspire and ignite sparks in you as it did in me. What started as a singular thought has blossomed into a universe of ideas ready for you to explore. Each chapter is a new adventure awaiting your discovery. It's packed with insights and nuggets of wisdom, all wrapped up in a way that makes you feel as if we're having a heart- to-heart over coffee. As you flip through these pages, I encourage you to engage with the content. Take notes, scribble your thoughts in the margins, and allow the ideas to bounce around your head like joyous fireworks. I truly want this to be a collaborative experience. Think of it as if you're joining me in this dialogue; your perspectives matter just as much as the words on the page.

Life has a funny way of throwing curveballs, and I've faced my fair share of challenges while putting this book together. But that struggle shaped the narrative and gave me the grit to push through. I faced moments where I questioned everything, wondering if I was really capable of conveying my visions. Yet, here I stand, heart racing with excitement and nerves as this book finds its way to you. You are my reason for pouring my soul into every single word!

In each story, you'll find a thread that connects us all, exploring themes that transcend borders and cultures. This book is like a vibrant mosaic made from the diverse pieces of our existence. I want to challenge you, inspire you, and set the stage for self-discovery, because trust me when I say the journey you're about to embark on is all about uncovering your spark.

So, let's not dawdle around! Let's jump headfirst into the intriguing content that lies ahead. I genuinely hope that as you read through these stories, you'll feel energized, captivated, and perhaps even transformed. Keep an open mind and heart, and allow this book to resonate within you.

Are you ready to dive deep into the magic of words? Trust me; you won't regret it! There's a treasure trove of ideas waiting for you, so buckle up and get ready for an unforgettable ride through the very fabric of what it means to be human.

Thank you for letting me share this incredible journey with you; I can't wait for you to discover what's in store. So grab a cozy spot, your favorite drink, and let's make some magic happen together.

With all my excitement,
Prof. Michael T. Adenitire

———— Chapter 1 ————

THE NAKED TRUTH

THE NAKED TRUTH

Defining Intimacy

Intimacy is often seen as a simple word, one that evokes images of physical closeness—perhaps the gentle brush of skin against skin, or the electric charge that travels between bodies nearby. However, intimacy runs far deeper than the physical realm. It is an intricate tapestry woven from emotional threads that bind partners together, creating a safe space where vulnerability can thrive. In this exploration, we will distinguish between physical and emotional intimacy, uncovering the profound depth of connection that lies in being truly intimate with another person.

The Nature of Intimacy

At its core, intimacy is about closeness. It is a bond that forms between partners, characterized by trust, openness, and a willingness to expose one's true self. To many, the idea of being intimate conjures thoughts of sexual relationships; however, this is only one facet of intimacy. When exploring the broader concept, one must acknowledge the significance of emotional intimacy, which encompasses the emotional sharing, security, and profound connection that partners experience with one another.

Physical intimacy may manifest in various ways—kissing, holding hands, hugging, and most certainly, engaging in sexual activity. These physical expressions often serve as the outward face of deeper emotional bonds. However, it is emotional intimacy that serves as the foundation upon which physical intimacy can thrive. Emotional intimacy is characterized by mutual understanding, supportive listening, and shared experiences that foster connection.

Consider the narrative of Sarah and Mark, a couple who faced their share of challenges in defining their intimate connections. In the beginning stages of their relationship, they found it easy to express their desires physically. The thrill of new love was exhilarating, and their passion for each other was palpable. They embraced each other in fervent kisses, exploring the physicality of intimacy at every turn. Yet, as time passed and routines seeped into their lives, Sarah realized that their connection began to diminish.

"I thought physical intimacy was enough," Sarah confided during a discussion about their relationship. "But as we moved through life together, I felt like something was missing. We were physically close, but emotionally, we had built walls around ourselves."

Mark echoed her sentiments, recalling a time when he felt exposed in their relationship. "There were evenings when we lay next to each other, engaged in our thoughts, and I yearned for a deeper connection. It wasn't that I didn't love her; I just felt a gap we needed to bridge."

This reflection captures the nuance between physical and emotional intimacy. It is through emotional intimacy that couples can attain a level of understanding that allows them to strip away the layers that shield their vulnerabilities. Mark and Sarah's journey illuminated the importance of delving into the emotional aspects of their relationship, leading them to foster a more profound intimacy.

The Vulnerability of True Intimacy

Vulnerability is often perceived as a liability, a risk that can lead to emotional harm. However, in the realm of intimacy, vulnerability is the key that unlocks deeper connections. It requires partners to relinquish control and embrace the inherent uncertainty that accompanies emotional exposure. The act of being vulnerable offers couples the opportunity to experience each other wholly and unapologetically—an endeavor that can be simultaneously daunting and exhilarating.

Through their shared vulnerability, couples can unveil their innermost fears, desires, and insecurities, creating an environment where they feel safe in their partner's presence. Emotional intimacy thrives on this kind of risk-taking, and when it is rewarded with understanding and acceptance, it solidifies the bond between partners.

Take the story of Lisa and David, who learned the importance of vulnerability in their relationship after navigating some turbulent waters. Following a significant life change—a job loss for David—Lisa noticed her partner retreating into himself. Concerned for him, she felt the weight of his silence pressing against their connection.

"I wanted to reach out, but I was scared he'd push me away," she said, recalling that challenging time. "I realized that if I didn't step out of my comfort zone, we'd drift further apart." Gathering her courage, she approached David one evening, hoping to breach the gap that had formed.

"Why are you pulling away from me?" she asked gently, her voice trembling slightly. "I'm here for you, and I want to help, but I need you to open up." David hesitated at first, aware that he'd built a wall around his feelings. But looking into Lisa's eyes, he saw her willingness to embrace his vulnerability without judgment.

In that moment, David took a leap of faith. "I'm scared," he admitted. "I've never been this worried about my career, and that fear makes me feel inadequate." Lisa's acceptance of his fear and her willingness to listen created a safe space where vulnerability could bloom. As they shared their fears and emotions, their connection deepened; the walls crumbled, paving the way for intimacy to flourish.

Insights from Couples on Emotional Closeness

Many couples understand the intricacies of emotional intimacy, often sharing stories that illuminate their journeys of vulnerability and connection. Such narratives illuminate the essence of being genuinely close to another, emphasizing that intimacy thrives in an environment of acceptance and understanding.

One couple, Rachel and Tom, spoke candidly about the transformation of their relationship after they learned to embrace emotional closeness. They described an experience that shifted their perception of intimacy during a difficult season in their marriage, where life adjustments and stress took a toll on their connection.

"Together, we realized that intimacy wasn't just about the good times," Rachel shared. "It was about facing adversity as a unit, being there for each other when things got tough." Tom added, "During that challenging time, I learned that I didn't have to carry my burdens alone—I could lean on Rachel, and she could lean on me." In that realization, they found an intimacy that transcended physicality, deepened by emotional understanding and support.

Similarly, Cassandra and Ethan recounted their experience of navigating emotional intimacy within the framework of their hectic lives. With careers and parenthood demanding their attention, they had fallen into routines that neglected the emotional aspects of their connection.

"Every night felt like a checklist," Cassandra admitted. "Dinner, dishes, bedtime for the kids— there was hardly any time for us." Recognizing this disconnect, they made a mutual commitment to prioritize openness. They created an evening ritual of unplugging from devices and shared their thoughts about their day without distractions. This intentional practice allowed them to express their feelings, fears, and dreams, nourishing their emotional intimacy.

"The simple act of asking how each other's day went opened the door for so many deeper conversations," Ethan noted. "When we pause and listen to each other, the connection strengthens." Their experience underscores that busy life schedules do not have to diminish intimacy; rather, intentionality can reignite emotional closeness.

The Interplay Between Emotional and Physical Closeness

It is essential to recognize the interplay between emotional intimacy and physical closeness, as they complement and enhance one another. While physical intimacy can serve as a tangible expression of love, it is often the emotional foundation that breathes life into these physical interactions. A relationship rich in emotional intimacy is likely to foster more meaningful physical expressions.

In the case of Laura and Jake, their journey highlighted the mutual reinforcement of emotional and physical intimacy. Initially captivated by each other's physical attributes, they soon discovered that the initial spark alone wasn't sufficient to sustain their relationship. After a series of heart-to-heart conversations, they intentionally carved out time to cultivate their emotional closeness, which positively influenced their physical connection.

"After we started talking and sharing more about our lives, it was like a light bulb went on," Laura reflected. "I felt closer to him emotionally, and that translated to a new level of physical connection." Jake concurred, stating, "It was no longer just about attraction—there was a depth to our intimacy that made physical moments feel electric."

Their experience illustrates that emotional intimacy lays the groundwork for physical expressions of love, creating a cycle of closeness where each aspect reinforces the other. This reciprocal relationship serves as a reminder that establishing and nurturing emotional bonds is critical to the overall intimacy within a partnership.

The Transformation of Intimacy over Time

As relationships progress, the dynamics of intimacy evolve. New stages of life, such as marriage, parenthood, and career changes, can influence both emotional and physical intimacy. Couples must navigate these transitions to ensure their bond remains intact amidst the shifting landscape.

Sarah and Mark's story illustrates how different stages of life can introduce new dimensions to intimacy. Years after their initial concerns about emotional closeness emerged, they found themselves navigating the complexities of parenting. Initiating candid conversations about their fears, desires, and expectations around parenting helped them maintain their emotional connection.

"We recognized quickly that if we didn't talk about our challenges, we would become isolated in our struggles," said Mark. "Parenthood is rewarding, but it can be so challenging, and we needed to be open about our feelings." This wisdom emphasizes the dynamic nature of intimacy, where relational needs must be adapted and honored as life changes present new challenges and joys.

In another example, Lisa and David reflected on how their emotional connection transformed after they became parents. While they once prioritized spontaneous romantic gestures, the demands of parenting required them to be intentional about nurturing intimacy in a new way. They began scheduling regular 'date nights' to reconnect and prioritize their emotional and physical closeness.

"Creating that time for just us was critical," confessed Lisa. "Those moments allowed us to rediscover our intimacy and share our joys and challenges as partners and parents." Their experience reveals that even as relationships change, finding ways to nurture intimacy remains essential.

Cultivating Intimacy through Listening and Understanding.

To foster intimacy in a relationship, couples must prioritize communication. This involves not only expressing needs and desires but also actively listening to each other. Listening with empathy and understanding allows partners to cultivate a deeper connection, inviting vulnerability into the relationship.

Anastasia and Samuel shared their insights on how empathetic listening transformed their relationship. "I'd often be focused on my own feelings without realizing I wasn't truly hearing Samuel," Anastasia shared. "Once I worked to really listen, things changed dramatically." Samuel added, "It felt like a weight was lifted when I knew she was genuinely trying to understand me."

Together, they realized that the act of listening—understanding each other's thoughts and emotions—enhanced their emotional intimacy. It fostered a sense of safety and understanding, encouraging both partners to be more open and vulnerable.

Conclusion

Intimacy is a multifaceted aspect of relationships that extends beyond physicality. It encompasses emotional closeness, vulnerability, and mutual understanding, nurturing a connection that thrives on acceptance. The stories of couples embarking on their journeys of intimacy reveal the richness that comes from being emotionally connected and transparent. As individuals work towards defining their intimacy, they must recognize the dynamic interplay between physical and emotional closeness—cultivating both aspects to create a strong and resilient bond.

Through intentional communication, vulnerability, and empathetic listening, couples can build a foundation of intimacy that will withstand the tests of time. True intimacy offers a sanctuary where partners can experience being truly seen and accepted, allowing them to embrace their authentic selves while deepening their connection with one another.

Cultural Perspectives

Cultural perspectives on intimacy are as diverse as the world's many societies, each with its own set of beliefs, practices, and expectations surrounding sexual and emotional closeness. Intimacy, in its various forms, is not an isolated experience; rather, it is deeply intertwined with cultural narratives and social norms that shape how individuals connect with one another. In exploring this intricate relationship between culture and intimacy, we can gain insight into the profound impact that sociocultural context has on our personal lives and relationships.

Historically, intimacy has often been conceptualized differently across regions and civilizations. For instance, traditional Western perspectives on intimacy have typically emphasized individualism, viewing relationships primarily as personal choices and expressions of love. In contrast, many non-Western cultures may approach intimacy through a collectivist lens, where family ties and communal bonds play a vital role in shaping individual relationships. This cultural divergence presents a rich tapestry of understanding that highlights how intimacy is perceived and practiced around the globe.

In some Indigenous cultures, intimacy is often viewed as a communal experience. Relationships are rarely confined to the couple; rather, they involve the extended family and community. For instance, many Native American tribes emphasize the importance of kinship ties in forming intimate connections. Couples are not just partners but rather members of a larger social fabric that supports and nurtures relationships. In this context, intimacy includes emotional support from family and the community, which reinforces the couple's bond.

Moving to the Eastern regions of the world, many cultures exhibit a different approach to intimacy, weaving it into the fabric of rituals and collective experiences. In Japan, for instance, intimacy can often be indirect, relying on subtle gestures and non-verbal communication. The cultural concept of "amae" is crucial here; it describes a sense of dependency and trusting intimacy unique to Japanese culture. Relationships often prioritize harmony and respect over overt expressions of affection, leading to a nuanced understanding of intimacy where emotional connection is fostered through shared experiences rather than explicit verbal affirmations.

Conversely, in countries such as India, intimacy is frequently entwined with traditional customs and societal structures. Arranged marriages are still common, and the intimate connection between partners is often developed over time rather than being an immediate outcome of romantic love. In these contexts, intimacy may initially be forged through familial expectations and shared values. Emotional closeness can grow as partners participate in shared rituals, festivals, and family interactions, which serve to gradually deepen their bond. This cultural perspective underscores that intimacy is not merely an individual endeavor but one that is influenced by familial and societal frameworks.

The role of gender in cultural perspectives on intimacy also cannot be overlooked. Across various societies, traditional gender roles often dictate how intimacy is navigated. In many cultures, women may be socialized to prioritize emotional intimacy, often being the primary caretakers of relationships, while men may be encouraged to adopt a more pragmatic approach. This dichotomy can lead to differing expectations and experiences of intimacy. For instance, in Mediterranean cultures, emotional expressions may be encouraged, allowing for passionate connections that involve close family ties, while in more conservative societies, men may feel pressure to uphold a stoic façade, suppressing emotional vulnerability.

When examining intimacy through a cultural lens, it's essential to include the perspectives of experts in sociology, anthropology, and psychology. These scholars highlight the implications of cultural norms on how couples experience and navigate intimacy. Dr. Ruth Westheimer, a renowned sex therapist, emphasizes that while cultural narratives can shape personal experiences, they are not definitive.

"Individuals often reinterpret their cultural narratives, creating their own definitions of intimacy based on personal experiences and emotional needs," she states. This perspective encourages individuals to seek emotionally fulfilling relationships that resonate with their values, rather than being bound strictly by cultural constructs. As such, intimacy becomes a fluid concept, capable of evolving as individuals negotiate their identities within the cultural frameworks that influence them.

In Africa, cultural practices surrounding intimacy can vary significantly across different regions and tribes. In many communities, communal living and shared responsibilities contribute to a unique understanding of relationship dynamics. Traditional practices such as "ukwenda," a cultural ritual among some tribes, emphasizes the importance of mutual understanding and respect in intimate relationships, often involving extensive family involvement in establishing and maintaining emotional bonds. This cultural framing often leads to an expectation of loyalty and mutual support that transcends the couple, extending to the community.

Similarly, in Latin America, where vibrant family ties and close-knit communities are central, intimacy is often expressed through warm familial relationships, deep emotional connections, and expressive communication styles. For many, love is intertwined with passionate celebration and connection; public displays of affection, both among couples and within families, are commonplace and socially accepted. A poignant example can be observed during family gatherings and celebrations, where music, dance, and shared meals play a vital role in nurturing intimacy. The concept of "familismo," prevalent in many Latin cultures, refers to the prioritization of family relationships, emphasizing loyalty and emotional closeness. In this context, intimacy is cultivated through shared experiences and collective involvement in each other's lives, creating a web of emotional connectivity that is often reinforced through cultural rituals.

Yet, a notable trend in contemporary society is the blending of cultural perspectives due to globalization and interconnectivity. As individuals from different backgrounds come together, cultural exchanges create new understandings of intimacy that transcend traditional boundaries. Couples today often draw from various cultural practices, integrating elements from their diverse heritages to create unique relational frameworks. This hybridization offers new ways to understand and express intimacy—opportunities to learn from one another's experiences and practices can enhance emotional connectivity, allowing for richer and deeper relationships.

Despite these cross-cultural encounters, it remains crucial to acknowledge the challenges that arise when navigating differing expectations of intimacy. Misunderstandings can stem from contrasting cultural narratives, leading to friction in relationships.

Issues of conforming to traditional gender roles, expectations surrounding sexual intimacy, and familial obligations can complicate the dynamics of intimate connections. Couples may find themselves at odds when their cultural backgrounds lead to differing priorities or methods of communication regarding emotional and sexual closeness.

This tension becomes particularly evident in multicultural relationships, where partners may face the challenge of reconciling their disparate cultural beliefs about intimacy. For instance, a couple where one partner comes from a culture that emphasizes emotional expression may struggle to engage with a partner whose background favors more reserved interactions. Navigating such differences requires open communication and a willingness to understand and appreciate the other's perspective.

In essence, cultural perspectives on intimacy are complex and multifaceted, encompassing a rich variety of beliefs, practices, and challenges. They inform how individuals experience love, sexual relations, and emotional connections, ultimately shaping the intimacy landscape around the globe. By acknowledging and exploring these diverse narratives, we can gain a deeper appreciation for our own backgrounds and the cultural influences that shape our intimate lives.

As we continue to investigate intimacy across cultures, it is essential for individuals to cultivate an awareness of how their cultural backgrounds influence their relational experiences. This awareness fosters understanding, empathy, and acceptance, allowing couples to create mutually fulfilling intimacy based on respect for their unique cultural perspectives.

Moreover, developing a nuanced understanding of intimacy across cultures can empower couples to embrace a shared journey of exploration and discovery. By learning from one another, they can craft their own definitions of intimacy that honor their unique experiences while respecting the rich tapestry of cultural narratives from which they draw. This process may involve challenging preconceived notions or stereotypes associated with intimacy rooted in their respective cultures, leading to deeper connections with their partners.

In conclusion, the cultural perspectives on intimacy profoundly shape our experiences of closeness, vulnerability, and emotional connection. By examining how various civilizations approach intimacy, we can develop a more inclusive understanding that honors diversity while promoting understanding and accountability in relationships. As we navigate the intricate landscape of intimacy, let us embark on our own journeys of introspection and connection, striving to cultivate depth and meaning in our relationships, no matter our cultural backgrounds.

The Importance of Being 'Naked'

In relationships, the concept of being 'naked' transcends mere physicality. It symbolizes a profound vulnerability that, when shared between partners, transforms the fabric of intimacy in a marriage. The act of being 'naked' can serve as a powerful metaphor for emotional exposure, suggesting that true closeness comes not from shared space or physical bodies, but from the courage to reveal one's inner self to another.

Emotional intimacy is the bedrock upon which sexual intimacy flourishes. Many couples often realize that their connection deepens not just when they disclose their desires but when they share their fears, dreams, and insecurities, laying bare the very essence of who they are. This depth of exposure fosters an atmosphere of safety, trust, and comfort, inviting open-hearted communication and leading to a fulfilling sexual relationship.

To illustrate this concept of emotional nakedness, let's explore a narrative from a couple, Mark and Lisa. They had been married for over a decade, and like many couples, they had experienced their fair share of ups and downs. Mark often felt that their intimacy had plateaued; their sexual encounters were routine, devoid of the passion they once shared. During a candid conversation one evening, Lisa surprised him with a revelation: "I feel like I can't share my true feelings with you, Mark. I worry about being judged when I express my fears about our relationship, and that keeps me from connecting with you fully."

This moment was pivotal for them. Mark realized that Lisa's fear of judgment was creating an emotional barrier, preventing them from experiencing the intimacy they both craved. Instead of reacting defensively, Mark took a step back and attempted to absorb Lisa's feelings. He shared his own vulnerabilities, admitting how he, too, often felt anxious about their connection. "I didn't realize I was putting pressure on you," he confessed. "I guess I felt similar fears but didn't know how to articulate them."

Through this exchange, Mark and Lisa recognized that their shared vulnerabilities had the potential to 'strip away' the emotional armor they wore. It led to heartfelt conversations about their desires and boundaries, effectively dismantling their barriers. As they gradually exposed their feelings to one another, they found that their regular sexual encounters sparked back to life with renewed vigor and passion. Being emotionally naked with each other enhanced not only their emotional connection but invigorated their sexual intimacy.

The importance of shared vulnerability is underscored further by another couple, Sarah and Tom, who faced the aftermath of a significant life change. After having their first child, Sarah experienced feelings of inadequacy and insecurities that she had never felt before. Unsure of how to convey her feelings to Tom, she withdrew emotionally. Feeling disconnected, Tom noticed Sarah's struggle but found himself at a loss for words.

One evening, as they sat together in the nursery, the dim light creating a gentle atmosphere, Tom gently asked Sarah, "What's going on, babe? You seem distant." Sarah hesitated, feeling the weight of her emotions pressing down on her. But with Tom's gentle encouragement, she eventually spoke up. "I feel lost. I thought I would embrace motherhood seamlessly, but I'm scared I'm failing. I don't want to let you down."

Tom's response was immediate and supportive. "You're not failing, Sarah. We're in this together. But I need you to share these things with me. I can't help unless I understand how you're feeling." This vulnerability led Sarah to open up about her fears, which included the fear of losing their intimate connection amid the chaos of parenting. This powerful discussion not only created emotional intimacy but reshaped their sexual relationship as they navigated their new roles as parents together, instilling a sense of partnership and unity that they had previously felt slipping.

Emotional nakedness undoubtedly facilitates deeper sexual intimacy. When both partners feel safe to express their innermost thoughts and experiences, it fosters an environment ripe for understanding and love. Shared vulnerability creates a ripple effect; when one partner dares to reveal their true self, the other often follows suit, establishing a mutual cycle of openness that enhances the relationship.

As couples cultivate this vulnerability, they often engage in deeper levels of physical affection that transition into a healthy sexual relationship. For example, consider Jennifer and Brian, who felt complacent in their sex life after years of routine. After a challenging conversation focused on emotional honesty, they began practicing intimacy rituals such as holding hands, eye contact, and continued conversations exploring what made them feel desired.

In the months that followed, this emotional exposure allowed Jennifer to reveal her fears surrounding physical intimacy— concerns linked to her body image after childbirth and Brian's struggles with confidence. Understanding these vulnerabilities enriched their relationship. Their sexual encounters transformed from mere physical engagements to profound experiences of connection, love, and acceptance. Emotional exposure translated into heightened sexual pleasure as they learned to navigate each other's emotional landscapes, requiring them to synchronize their physical and emotional desires.

Encouraging emotional exposure not only aids in improving sexual intimacy but also supports conflict resolution and overall relationship satisfaction. Couples equipped with enhanced communication skills and a willingness to be emotionally naked often find that they can approach conflicts constructive. Sandra and Mike realized this when their differing views on finances led to constant arguments. Rather than reverting to blame, they decided to engage in an emotionally open dialogue about their individual experiences regarding money upbringing and the anxieties it provoked in them.

As they shared their personal backgrounds surrounding finances, their understanding of each other deepened, allowing them to coordinate their spending and save together, transforming the conflict into a shared commitment. The emotional nakedness they practiced not only alleviated tensions in their financial discussions but also translated into more intimate experiences, sparking deeper discussions of their dreams and aspirations. This moment allowed for a rekindled sense of intimacy that they thought lost in mundane financial woes.

In order to cultivate emotional exposure and encourage couples to embrace vulnerability, developing practical exercises catered towards enhancing their emotional connection can be beneficial. Trust-building activities can commence with simple practices, such as dedicating time for open dialogue, where partners commit to sharing thoughts and feelings without judgment. Revisiting memories that engage emotional recollections can also deepen intimacy; take a walk down memory lane, share the impact of their first moments together, or discuss pivotal life-changing moments. Sharing these memories leads to richer conversations and an appreciation of each other's journeys.

Another exercise partners can engage in is the "vulnerability jar." Each partner writes down one fear, insecurity, or dream on a piece of paper and places it in a jar. The couple takes turns selecting a note and discussing what it means to them. Each discussion can act as a stepping stone to greater emotional exposure, poising the couple to identify their emotional landscapes with greater clarity.

Incorporating touch into the equation reinforces the notion of emotional nakedness. Physical affection such as hugging, cuddling, and gentle strokes played an integral role for couples like Megan and Ryan. They often expressed how physical gestures coupled with their emotional discussions created a symbiotic relationship, where one act of vulnerability opened the door to another. As they practiced sharing their worries and dreams, they made it a habit to engage in thoughtful physical touch, resulting in richer emotional and physical intimacy built on trust.

The importance of being emotionally naked extends beyond just improving sexual intimacy, serving as a critical foundation for overall relationship satisfaction and fulfillment. Emotional exposure enables couples not only to confront their worst fears and insecurities but also emerge on the other side hand in hand. This journey of vulnerability requires patience and understanding, yet couples swiftly find that the rewards profoundly outweigh the discomfort.

Furthermore, the significance of being 'naked' in emotional terms amplifies the concept of safety in a relationship. Creating a safe space for your partner to express feelings and insecurities cultivates resilience in both partners. Intimacy built on emotional exposure makes it easier for partners to navigate challenges, allowing them to lean on each other during difficulties while celebrating victories together.

Thus, the journey towards achieving deeper emotional and sexual intimacy is not only a romantic pursuit; but rather a fundamental aspect of building a lasting, intimately connected life together. Healthy intimacy means embracing vulnerability, choosing to be 'naked' with one another in deeper and more profound ways, allowing love to flourish beyond the physical norms and customs society imposes.

In conclusion, the metaphor of being naked encapsulates a transformative experience for couples. This shared vulnerability creates a unique and beautiful dance of intimacy, where emotional exposure leads to richer sexual experiences and a stronger emotional connection. As couples embark on this journey of honesty and openness, they discover that true intimacy is less about body exposure and more about the liberation found in revealing the depths of one's heart and soul to another.

—— Chapter 2 ——

BARRIERS TO CONNECTION

BARRIERS TO CONNECTION

Identifying Common Barriers

Intimacy is a vital aspect of a thriving relationship, yet many couples experience significant barriers that prevent them from connecting on a deeper level. Understanding these common obstacles is the first step in navigating the intricate dynamics of emotional and sexual closeness. In this subchapter, we will explore critical barriers to intimacy, such as fear of judgment, past traumas, and societal pressures. Through the lens of personal testimonials, we will examine how these issues manifest differently for each couple and provide insights into overcoming them.

Fear of Judgment

One of the most pervasive barriers to intimacy is the fear of judgment. This fear can take numerous forms, including concerns about how one's desires, body image, or vulnerabilities will be perceived by their partner. Couples often find themselves holding back from expressing their true feelings and desires, worrying that their partner may not accept them or may view them in a negative light. This can lead to a cycle of hesitance, where partners withdraw into themselves, creating only superficial connections.

For instance, consider the story of Lily and Mark. In their early years of marriage, Lily often felt self-conscious about her body, particularly after having children. She would shy away from intimacy, fearing that Mark would judge her harshly. "I would put on the lights just before we would be intimate, and that left me feeling exposed and judged," she shared. Mark had no idea of her struggles with self-image; to him, she was beautiful and desirable. However, her fear created distance between them, as she refrained from initiating intimacy.

Mark recalled, "I would try to tell her how beautiful I thought she was, but she never believed me. It wasn't until we attended a couple's retreat that she realized how negative thoughts about her body were becoming a barrier."

It was during those sessions that Lily learned strategies to combat her fear.

ngside other couples, she began recognizing that her feelings were not isolating; they were much more universal. The retreat provided a safe space for her to express her fears without judgment. Through exercises focused on vulnerability, she began to understand that true intimacy grows when partners feel safe to show their true selves, even their imperfections.

Past Traumas

Another poignant barrier to intimacy arises from past traumas. Individual traumatic experiences can profoundly shape one's ability to connect with others emotionally and sexually. When someone has been hurt or betrayed in the past, they may carry those memories into their current relationships, affecting their willingness to fully engage with their partner.

Carlos and Maria illustrate this point well. Carlos had experienced a painful betrayal in a previous relationship. He entered his relationship with Maria with a fear of being hurt again. "I found myself pushing her away, even subconsciously," he revealed. "Sometimes, I would withdraw or pull back when we were becoming close, out of fear that she would cheat on me like my ex." Maria, confused and hurt by his behavior, felt rejected anytime Carlos held back his affection. "I felt like I was always walking on eggshells," Maria shared. "I knew he loved me, but those moments of closeness terrified him. I couldn't understand why he wouldn't just let go."

To help navigate this challenge, Carlos sought therapy, both individually and as a couple. Through deeper exploration, he began to understand how his past traumas manifested as fear in his current relationship. He learned to communicate his needs and concerns to Maria, helping to build trust slowly. Maria, armed with this knowledge and understanding, was able to offer reassurance to Carlos, allowing him to feel safe in expressing his vulnerability.

This journey of healing is crucial not just for Carlos, but for many others who find themselves hindered by the weight of past experiences. Learning and recognizing how trauma can affect intimacy is a critical step in making informed choices about emotional closeness and trust.

Societal Pressures

Societal pressures also pose significant barriers to intimacy. The impacts of societal norms regarding relationships can dictate how individuals perceive their intimacy and sexual expectations. Cultural narratives about how a 'perfect relationship' should look can create unrealistic standards that many couples feel compelled to chase, often at the expense of genuine intimacy.

For example, Sarah and Jake felt societal pressure to maintain a certain image. Friends and family members often measured their relationship against a narrow view of success, making them feel inadequate when they faced challenges. "We were constantly comparing ourselves to social media couples who always seemed so happy and perfect," Sarah explained. "It made us question our own relationship and whether we were doing it right."

As a result, when Sarah and Jake faced ordinary marital challenges like disagreements or a decline in sexual desire, they felt like failures. Instead of fostering intimacy through open communication, they turned against each other, blaming themselves for not living up to the imagined standards.

"Instead of talking about the issues, we just started to silently resent each other," Jake admitted. "I thought that if we just didn't talk about our problems, they would just go away. But that just created more distance."

They eventually realized that the comparison was destroying their connection. Inspired to change, they sought to redefine intimacy within the context of their values and experiences. By discussing the pressures they felt and engaging in honest conversations about their relationship, they discovered that seeking validation externally only led to feelings of emptiness. Their focusnshifted towards nurturing their bond rather than molding it to an outside ideal, ultimately strengthening their intimacy.

Understanding Individual Contexts

The barriers of fear, trauma, and societal pressure can manifest uniquely within each relationship. It's crucial for couples to understand that what holds one person back may not be the same for their partner. Creating an open dialogue within the relationship allows couples to explore these barriers together, fostering greater understanding and empathy.

For instance, some couples may discover that while one partner struggles with fear of judgment, the other may be grappling with feelings of inadequacy stemming from past experiences. As partners explore these complexities together, they are more likely to develop strategies that help them both feel secure in their intimacy.

A poignant example comes from couples who have navigated intimacy after infidelity. For Robert and Jessica, the road to recovery was paved with the recognition of their individual barriers. Robert, who had cheated, had to confront his fears of vulnerability and rejection. Jessica, betrayed and heartbroken, had to work through her fear of being unlovable when faced with such trauma. Their shared journey of understanding emotions evolved into a newfound intimacy, transforming the very fabric of their relationship.

By identifying and discussing their barriers, Robert was able to express remorse while Jessica learned to communicate her needs for reassurance. Their willingness to embrace vulnerability became the cornerstone of rebuilding not only trust, but deeper emotional intimacy.

Taking the First Steps

The journey toward overcoming barriers to intimacy mirrors any other challenge couples face; it begins with awareness and communication. Acknowledging the presence of these barriers is the first step toward addressing and dismantling them. Couples can encourage one another to share their fears without judgment, allowing each partner a chance to voice their vulnerabilities. By creating sacred spaces, where there is no fear of judgment, couples can build a bridge to intimacy that can withstand the stressors of life.

One effective practice is to carve out regular time for emotional check-ins. During these moments, neither partner suggests solutions but instead focuses on being present. This intentional vulnerability can be eye-opening, providing insights into how their partner perceives past judgments and past experiences.

Another powerful tool is therapeutic modalities. Couples may consider engaging in therapy individually or as a team. Therapy creates a space for deeper exploration of issues like trauma and societal pressures. With the support of a professional, partners can learn how to better express their opinions and navigate the complexities of their emotional dynamics.

Embracing Vulnerability as Strength

Ultimately, it is essential to embrace vulnerability as a strength rather than a weakness. By acknowledging their barriers, couples can take deliberate steps toward fostering closeness and intimacy. Understanding that it is not just individual struggles that matter, but also how these experiences affect their relationship, provides the foundation upon which intimacy can thrive.

Through dedication, practice, and a willingness to confront fears, past traumas, and societal pressures, couples can cultivate a deep and abiding intimacy. Creating this bond equips partners to navigate the complexities of their union, addressing barriers in a constructive manner, and paving the way for a lasting intimate connection.

Looking ahead, remaining attuned to the evolving nature of these barriers will enable couples to continually fortify their emotional and physical bonds. The journey toward deeper intimacy is ongoing and enriching, marked by shared experiences and a commitment to overcoming adversity together.

Overcoming Fear and Trauma

Emily and Jake had enjoyed a blissful relationship for the first few years of their marriage. Their bond was characterized by laughter, shared dreams, and mutual respect. But as they approached their fifth anniversary, things suddenly changed. Emily began to withdraw. A few months later, Jake discovered the reason: Emily had faced a traumatic event in her past that she had never shared with him. The memories had resurfaced, invading their intimacy like a dark shadow, casting fear over their once-vibrant connection.

Emily's trauma was not something she had hidden; rather, she had compartmentalized it. In her mind, she believed that discussing it would shatter the idyllic world she and Jake had created together. But her avoidance soon spiraled into emotional withdrawal, leaving Jake feeling helpless and confused.

After a particularly painful night of silence, when Emily had refused to be intimate with him or even share her feelings, Jake gently insisted that they seek help. Reluctantly, Emily agreed. They found a therapist specialized in trauma and intimacy. This decision, while daunting, marked the beginning of their journey toward healing.

In therapy, it became increasingly clear that Emily's trauma was deeply entwined with her ability to connect intimately. As they delved deeper, Emily learned that her fear wasn't just about her experience but also a fear of vulnerability. She feared the possibility of rejection—of sharing deeply personal parts of herself and being met with disdain or misunderstanding. Jake, on the other hand, had his own reservations. He feared that he might not know how to support Emily effectively, that somehow he could deepen her pain instead of helping her heal.

As part of their therapeutic journey, they engaged in exercises focusing on communication and emotional connection. The therapist guided them through exercises that helped identify their fears and express them without judgment. They learned to hold space for each other—to listen to the unsaid and understand that fear could coexist with love.

As they tackled Emily's fears, Jake also found the courage to voice his concerns. He shared how her withdrawal sometimes made him feel rejected and unworthy, causing his own fears to surface. Together, they worked to create a safe environment where both of their vulnerabilities could flourish without fear of rejection.

Simultaneously, they learned the importance of reassurance. One particular session stood out to them when their therapist guided them in an exercise of affirmations. They took turns affirming each other's strengths and expressing gratitude for their presence in each other's lives. Through these exercises, it became clear that positive reinforcement could serve as a bridge over treacherous waters of fear and doubt.

Furthermore, they explored the concept of pacing in intimacy. Emily found comfort in knowing that intimacy didn't have to conform to typical timelines. Instead, it could be approached with care and tenderness, allowing her to set the pace. This realization transformed their physical connection, allowing for a more profound emotional bond prior to sex. The pressure to perform or achieve intimacy became secondary to the goal of simply being present with each other.

As weeks turned into months, they began to encounter tangible progress. Emily told Jake that sharing her story—her fears and her trauma—felt like shedding a heavy blanket that had dulled their colors. They established rituals—like date nights—where they could focus solely on each other without the oppressive weight of the outside world or the distractions of daily responsibilities.

One evening, with a soft glow of candlelight and soothing music in the background, Emily finally opened up. She shared her experience in vivid detail, tears streaming down her cheeks as she recounted the fear she had lived with for so long. Jake listened intently, his heart aching for her pain but filled with admiration that she had found the strength to share such a burden with him.

In return, Jake shared his feelings of helplessness and the guilt he felt for not recognizing what Emily had been going through. This exchange marked a turning point in their relationship—a moment that united them in their vulnerabilities rather than dividing them. They began to view their fears not as insurmountable obstacles, but as opportunities for deeper understanding and connection.

As they navigated this journey, they also required ongoing encouragement and guidance. They were fortunate to attend a couple's retreat designed to help partners overcome trauma and foster intimacy. This retreat provided a safe space for couples to learn together, share stories, and support one another. Their facilitator emphasized the importance of creating rituals of connection, encouraging couples to cultivate daily habits that nurtured their intimacy.

In one exercise, participants were invited to share their "healing words"—phrases that resonated with comfort and hope. Jake articulated that nurturing should be at the core of their interactions. Emily highlighted the importance of safety, where she felt she could fully express her needs without fear of misunderstanding. By verbalizing these words, they could create a shared language of love that would serve to reinforce their bond.

Support from the outside world also played a crucial role in their progress. Emily found solace in talking to friends who had experienced similar traumas, letting her know that she wasn't alone. She felt empowered every time a friend opened up about their mental health struggles, and she began to realize that vulnerability is often a gateway to strength.

Jake also connected with peers who had dealt with the repercussions of their partners' fears—men who had faced the overwhelming challenge of wanting to help but feeling ill-equipped to do so. These friendships fostered an understanding of mutual support, proving that they weren't alone in their struggles.

As they spent more time exploring their emotional intimacy and healing together, it became clear that their relationship had transformed. They learned that healing was not linear—there were ups and downs—but they confronted challenges side by side. They integrated check-ins into their daily routine, allowing for moments of honesty about their emotional states. They established codes that signaled distress without putting pressure on each other to produce immediate solutions.

One rainy afternoon, while contemplating their journey, Emily shared how far they had come. "It's like peeling back layers," she said. "Each time we face another fear, we uncover something beautiful. I feel like I can finally be myself with you." Jake reached for her hand and smiled, knowing this was just the beginning of many conversations to come.

Upon realizing their profound emotional connection, their physical intimacy began to flourish. Emily's trauma no longer dictated the terms of their relationship. Instead, it became a shared narrative of resilience and growth. They learned to embrace their differences and their individual stories, nurturing compassion and understanding for each other's journeys. The weight of unvoiced fears gradually lifted, giving way to the liberating sense of connection.

Their experience became an emblem of hope for couples engulfed in the throes of fear and trauma. Emily and Jake often shared their story in workshops, emphasizing the importance of vulnerability and starting difficult conversations.

In some workshops, they engaged attendees in exercises aimed at rebuilding trust and intimacy. One exercise called "The Bridge" encouraged participants to support each other in facing a fear—be it a fear of rejection, intimacy, or discussing past trauma. Couples would take turns standing on one end of the room, voicing their fear while their partner remained at the other end. Then, the partner would be invited to walk toward the other person, creating a physical representation of bridging the gap between shared vulnerabilities.

As they guided couples through this exercise, Emily and Jake witnessed transformations. Couples would break down barriers, share truths, and embrace the unfiltered beauty of their stories. They became a beacon of hope, inspiring those who felt isolated by their experiences.

To further their journey, they began creating an online community, where couples could anonymously share their stories or seek support. The platform became a haven for people longing to be heard and understood. On weekends, they hosted virtual support groups where couples could talk openly about their concerns, fears, and triumphs. A consistent theme emerged: fear can be an insidious barrier to intimacy, but with open communication and a willingness to confront past traumas, healing is entirely possible.

Ultimately, their story serves as a reminder that overcoming fear and trauma in relationships is not merely about achieving an end goal. Rather, it's a continuous journey—one that requires unwavering commitment and a shared understanding that love thrives when nurtured in an environment of honesty and vulnerability. The bonds they formed together, the resilience they cultivated as a couple, and the connection they established serve as testament that even the heaviest burdens can be lifted when faced together.

As Jake stated during their final workshop, "Intimacy is not just about the absence of fear, but about the courage to lean into those fears together. It's about strength in vulnerability, and showing up for one another, time and time again."

The lessons learned through their journey echo throughout their lives—serve as a living testament to both the pain and the promise of love in the face of shadows.

Through community support, shared platforms, and genuine connections, couples like Emily and Jake continue to inspire others. No matter the past, healing and thriving intimately together are possible and achievable, shaping a future filled with love, understanding, and authentic intimacy.

Challenging Societal Norms

Intimacy is a multifaceted concept that transcends the realm of physical closeness and dives deep into emotional connections, shared experiences, and mutual understanding. However, societal norms often impose limitations on intimacy, dictating how relationships should function and how affection should be expressed. These expectations can create barriers, making it difficult for couples to connect on deeper levels. This subchapter aims to critique these societal norms and explores ways for couples to actively redefine their relationships to foster genuine intimacy.

From a young age, individuals are exposed to societal expectations about romantic relationships. Movies, literature, and even conversations within families send clear messages about what is 'normal' in a relationship. Many of these messages emphasize conventionality, often portraying the ideal relationship as one devoid of conflict, rich with passion, and characterized by traditional gender roles. Such representations can set unrealistic standards and create a sense of obligation that couples feel they must abide by.

This societal lens can cloud the perception of what true intimacy looks like and how it can be authentically expressed.

Society often promotes a narrow view of intimacy that prioritizes physicality over emotional connection. This perspective leads many couples to believe that intimacy equates to sexual activity. However, intimacy encompasses a wider spectrum that includes trust, transparency, and emotional vulnerability. When societal expectations confine intimacy to the bedroom, couples may overlook the importance of nurturing their emotional connection, which is foundational to a fulfilling relationship.

Consider the impact of social media, where carefully curated images and posts often depict idealized relationships — perfect couples enjoying romantic getaways or triumphantly celebrating anniversaries with extravagant gifts. Such portrayals can foster feelings of inadequacy among couples who may not experience the same level of connection or excitement. This comparison culture can lead to neglecting the necessary work of building genuine intimacy, as couples may find themselves caught in a cycle of trying to meet these unrealistic expectations instead of focusing on their unique relationship dynamics.

In many cultures, there are prescriptive narratives about how love should be expressed, with gender roles often reinforcing these expectations. For instance, women may feel pressured to be more emotional and nurturing, while men are often expected to display strength and stoicism. These outdated notions can stifle open communication, leading partners to hide their true feelings or suppress their needs. As a result, couples may become trapped in roles that limit their ability to connect authentically, hindering intimacy.

The first step in challenging these societal norms is for couples to recognize and name the beliefs and expectations that shape their understandings of intimacy. This self-awareness lays the groundwork for redefining their relationships. Partners should engage in open, honest discussions about their individual beliefs about intimacy, derived largely from societal influences. This dialogue allows both partners to express their feelings and concerns while also highlighting differing perspectives on intimacy.

Once a couple is aware of the external influences impacting their relationship, they can work collaboratively to redefine what intimacy means for them. This process often requires challenging cultural narratives that prescribe certain behaviors or attitudes as the norm. Individual comfort levels with vulnerability, affection, and communication styles must be explored, allowing couples to create a shared definition of intimacy that feels authentic to both.

Adopting a growth mindset is essential on this journey of redefinition. Embracing the idea that intimacy can evolve and change as the relationship deepens can liberate couples from rigid expectations. Rather than viewing intimacy through a static lens or comparing themselves to societal ideals, couples can learn to appreciate the unique aspects of their bond. Open dialogue about fears, desires, and experiences can promote resilience and adaptability in the face of societal pressures.

In redefining their relationship, couples can also explore non-traditional expressions of intimacy that resonate with them. For example, some may find that physical touch and sexual connection come naturally, while others might prioritize emotional and verbal intimacy. Integrating practices that foster this deeper connection, such as practicing active listening, sharing stories about their lives, and engaging in shared activities that promote bonding, can lead to profound shifts in their dynamic.

Experts suggest that prioritizing the quality of interactions over the frequency of intimate moments can enhance feelings of closeness.

Encouraging couples to engage in meaningful conversations, spend quality time together, and express affection outside of sexual encounters nurtures a sense of security and trust. As intimacy evolves beyond the constraints of societal expectations, couples can foster a connection that feels genuine and fulfilling based on their unique needs.

Moreover, couples should continuously reassess and communicate their evolving needs and desires, as intimacy is not a one-time achievement, but rather a continuous journey. By establishing rituals or regular check-ins to discuss their relationship's dynamics, couples can stay attuned to each other's emotional landscapes. This practice not only deepens their connection but also creates an environment of mutual respect and understanding, reinforcing the foundation of lasting intimacy.

Challenging societal norms around intimacy also involves rejecting shame and the stigma often attached to certain expressions of love. Courageously addressing patterns of intimacy that may deviate from traditional norms, such as non-monogamous relationships, same-sex partnerships, or open arrangements, can empower couples to embrace their authentic selves. These relationships often cultivate deep levels of connection and intimacy through the sheer act of challenging societal expectations together.

To foster a culture that embraces diverse definitions and expressions of intimacy, couples should also seek out community resources, couples' groups, or therapeutic support systems.

Learning from others who have navigated similar challenges can provide valuable insights and encourage a broader understanding of intimacy. By building a support network that values individuality and authenticity, couples gain the confidence to dismantle limiting societal norms.

Intimacy is, at its core, about connection and mutual understanding. Couples become more skilled at navigating the intricacies of intimacy when they openly confront and reject societal expectations. This conscious approach transforms their relationship into one where individuality and vulnerability are celebrated rather than stifled. Empowered by this newfound clarity, couples can forge deeper connections rooted in trust, honesty, and respect.

As couples redefine their relationships, their journey can become a source of inspiration for others seeking deeper intimacy. By demonstrating the courage to challenge societal pressures, they inspire a broader movement toward authenticity in relationships. This willingness to be vulnerable, to embrace differences, and to reject expectations can ultimately enrich not only their lives but also those of others watching from the sidelines.

In conclusion, challenging societal norms around intimacy requires self-awareness, open communication, a willingness to redefine relationships, and the courage to embrace change. As couples learn to navigate the complexities of intimacy beyond the rigid confines of societal expectations, they unlock the potential for authentic connections that are unique to their experiences. Through empathy, respect, and a commitment to mutual understanding, they can foster a bond that flourishes, ensuring that both partners feel valued and fulfilled. Ultimately, it is this dedication to redefining intimacy that paves the way for deeper, more meaningful connections that withstand the pressures of modern society.

------ Chapter 3 ------

THE LANGUAGE OF LOVE

THE LANGUAGE OF LOVE

Communicating Needs

In the intricate tapestry of intimate relationships, the ability to communicate needs effectively stands as a critical thread. Conversations that center around desires and boundaries can transform a relationship, fostering deeper connections and encouraging a safety net where vulnerability thrives. Yet, many couples find themselves stumbling over these conversations. Stepping into dialogue about personal desires can feel daunting, but approaching it with clarity and compassion can yield profound results.

Communication is foundational in any relationship, yet when it comes to discussing intimacy, its significance heightens dramatically. The human experience is rich with desires—physical, emotional, and intellectual. When these desires go unexpressed, they can manifest as frustration, misunderstandings, or a sense of disconnection. Therefore, understanding how to articulate needs can lead to not only improved intimacy but also a healthier overall relationship dynamic.

To begin, it is essential to recognize that communication is not merely about speaking; it involves active listening, empathy, and understanding. Verbalizing one's needs is just the first step. The way that we express ourselves, the timing, and the manner in which we engage our partner can significantly influence the outcomes of these conversations.

A common framework adopted by many couples when addressing their needs is the use of "I" statements. This communication tool shifts the focus from blaming or pointing fingers to expressing personal feelings and desires. For instance, instead of saying, "You never initiate intimacy anymore," one could rephrase to, "I feel distant from you lately, and I miss our intimate moments together." This technique fosters understanding and prevents the partner from becoming defensive.

When Sarah and Tom started focusing on "I" statements, they noticed a remarkable shift in their discussions about intimacy. Sarah shared how she felt when Tom would come home tired and uninterested in cuddling. Instead of accusing him of neglecting her needs, she expressed her feelings of loneliness, sparking a dialogue about how they could create more space for intimacy even amid busy schedules.

Encouraging healthy dialogue means preparing for it. Setting aside time specifically for these conversations can help both partners feel more at ease. Casual, offhand remarks during a stressful moment are far less effective than setting a dedicated time to talk. Creating a routine around discussing desires can be beneficial. Whether it's during a weekly coffee date or a quiet evening at home, establishing a safe emotional space sets the groundwork for meaningful exchange. Another strategy for effective communication involves being specific about what one needs. Broad statements can lead to confusion and misinterpretation. Instead of saying, "I need more from you," one should dive deeper into specifics: "I would love it if we could spend some time together without distractions on Friday nights so we can reconnect."

Moreover, approaching these conversations with a sense of curiosity can be immensely productive. Instead of assuming that you know what your partner wants, ask open-ended questions. This can lead not only to a broader understanding of each other's desires but may also introduce new dimensions to your intimacy. For example, asking, "What are some things you've been wanting to try together?" opens the door for exploration and creativity.

Consider Jake and Melissa, who found their intimacy waning over time. They decided to dedicate one evening a month to explore new activities together. By asking each other what they wanted to try, they rediscovered shared interests and reignited their desire for each other through playful exploration. These evenings evolved into intimate, treasured moments where both learned to communicate their desires in a supportive environment.

Setting boundaries is an equally important component of discussing desires. While communicating what one wants is great, understanding personal limits and being truthful about them protects both partners. Open discussions about boundaries can prevent misunderstandings and build trust. Each person's comfortability levels should be respected, allowing space for individual expressions of intimacy.

Anna, recounting her journey of self-discovery, realized that she had been compromising her own boundaries in her relationship with Mark. By initiating an earnest conversation about what she was comfortable with, she fostered an environment where both could express their boundaries freely. This honesty deepened their connection and resulted in an intimacy that was not only enjoyable but also respectful and fulfilling.

It's vital to remember that discussing needs is not a one-time conversation, but rather an ongoing dialogue. As relationships evolve, so do individual desires and boundaries. Regularly checking in with each other encourages partners to stay attuned to changes, fostering intimacy and connection over the long haul. Those continual check-ins, where both partners openly discuss feelings, transformations, and needs, create a culture of adaptability in the relationship.

Affirming each other during these exchanges is equally crucial. Celebrating small victories, expressing gratitude for shared moments, and reassuring each other can reinforce the emotional connection that intimacy thrives on. A simple "I appreciate you sharing that" can be a powerful affirmation that encourages further communication.

While it may be tempting to dwell on the problems that hinder intimacy, it's important to focus also on the strengths of the relationship. Identifying what works well can lend confidence to both partners and provide a solid foundation for approaching difficult conversations. Couples might find it beneficial to share their favorite moments of intimacy, reflecting on what made those instances special. This positive reinforcement not only boosts morale but allows each partner to explore aspects of intimacy they may want to engage in more deeply.

Moreover, empathy plays a critical role in navigating discussions about desires and boundaries. In order to communicate effectively, it is essential to truly listen to what one's partner is saying. Being responsive to their feelings fosters an emotional climate where each person feels valued and understood. When partners approach one another with empathy, they can navigate conversations with less defensiveness and more openness.

In moments of conflict or misunderstanding, taking a step back to practice empathy can yield breakthroughs. For instance, if an individual feels rejected when their partner is unable to fulfill a desire, reframing this reaction through the lens of empathy can help both partners better understand each other's perspectives and emotions. Taking the time to step into the other's shoes allows space for resolution and mutual understanding.

Additionally, utilizing non-verbal communication is an often-overlooked aspect of discussing intimacy. Body language, tone of voice, and eye contact can convey messages just as powerfully as words. Couples should be aware of their physical expressions when discussing intimate needs and desires. A gentle touch, open posture, or warm gaze can signal an inviting space for discussion, while crossed arms or avoiding eye contact may create barriers.

As we explore this delicate dance of communication further, it's essential to address those magical moments of intimacy when everything aligns perfectly, where partners feel deeply connected without the messiness of words. These moments often bridge the gaps created in prior conversations around needs. Engaging in shared activities that both partners enjoy can deepen bonds and reinforce their emotional connection.

Lisa and Rob found that by incorporating rituals such as dance classes or cooking together, they learned to communicate their needs without always relying on words. They became more responsive to each other's cues, developing an intuitive understanding of each other's desires. This shared experience enriched their relationship, creating a safe environment where they felt comfortable articulating their individual needs.

It's also important to embrace the fact that some conversations will be awkward or uncomfortable. This does not negate their importance. Acknowledging the discomfort of exposing one's vulnerabilities can be empowering. Partners can set the stage for a more successful dialogue by approaching the subject with humor or gentleness, easing the tension that accompanies difficult topics.

Additionally, couples may sometimes benefit from seeking external support, such as couples therapy or workshops focused on communication skills. Professional guidance can provide tools for couples to master their communication styles and address intimacy conflicts in a constructive way. Facilitated workshops often promote active participation and practical exercises that encourage partners to confront their expressions of desire and boundaries together.

To further illustrate the importance of effectively communicating needs, let's explore a few real-life scenarios.

Scenario One:

Jessica and Eric had been together for several years but found that intimacy was dwindling. Jessica felt frustrated but was unsure how to approach the topic without hurting Eric's feelings. After some encouragement from friends, she drafted a letter to Eric that outlined her feelings and her desire for deeper intimacy. When they finally sat down to discuss the letter, the conversation flowed naturally. Eric was grateful for her honesty, which led to discussions about their different intimacy needs. Eventually, they were able to establish regular date nights and explore new activities, which reignited the spark in their relationship.

Scenario Two:

In another instance, Natalie had been resistant to mentioning her need for connection following their recent move. She feared that her partner, Ryan, would feel overwhelmed by change. During a quiet evening, she chose to voice her feelings, expressing how isolated she felt without family nearby. Ryan was relieved to hear her honesty and expressed his own insecurities about the move. The couple then created a plan to connect with local friends, fulfilling Natalie's needs for companionship and nurturing Ryan's desire for connection as well.

Both scenarios highlight the power of clear, open communication in addressing intimacy needs. By confronting difficult conversations with honesty and empathy, couples can foster a vibrant partnership grounded in trust and understanding.

Building a thriving intimate relationship requires ongoing commitment, remaining aware of each partner's desires and needs. By engaging in intentional conversations, couples can maintain a strong emotional connection. This blueprint of open communication allows respect for boundaries while aligning their shared experiences, ultimately nourishing intimacy.

As relationships progress, diligently managing communication becomes a vital ingredient in sustaining intimacy. Practicing these principles in daily interactions encourages a culture of openness that signifies respect for both parties involved. When partners learn to share their needs freely, listen intently, and explore desires with a genuine sense of care, they create an emotional sanctuary where love can flourish solidly.

In conclusion, clear communication shapes the foundation of intimate relationships. Cultivating awareness of one's own needs and learning to express them articulately while ensuring that partners feel comfortable doing the same can pave the way toward richly fulfilling intimacy. Prioritizing these conversations not only enhances desire but solidifies emotional connections, leading to a more profound and lasting partnership. Through effective communication, a thrilling dance of closeness blossoms, where couples can be both courageous and vulnerable in their shared journey.

Listening With Empathy

Listening is often viewed as a passive activity, a mere act of hearing words without truly engaging with the speaker. However, in the realm of intimacy, listening transforms into a powerful tool—a bridge that connects partners in understanding, trust, and vulnerability. In this exploration of empathy in listening, we will dive into what it means to listen actively, how empathy enhances this process, and offer practical exercises to foster this vital skill in intimate conversations.

Understanding Active Listening

At its core, active listening is the act of fully concentrating, understanding, responding, and remembering what is being said. Unlike simple hearing, which involves the perception of sound, active listening requires engagement and intention. This is especially important in conversations with our partners, where emotions often run high and the stakes feel significant. Active listening involves several crucial components:

1. Attention: This means being fully present in the moment. It requires the listener to set aside distractions, both external and internal, and focus solely on their partner.

2. Reflection: After listening to what the partner has said, reflecting back with paraphrases like, "What I'm hearing is..." shows not only engagement but also a genuine effort to understand.

3. Clarification: Asking questions to clear up any ambiguities can help ensure both partners are on the same page.

4. Validation: Acknowledging the partner's feelings, even if one does not entirely agree, helps build safety in sharing vulnerable thoughts.

5. Response: The final step involves responding thoughtfully, which encourages further conversation.

The Power of Empathy

Empathy takes active listening a step further. It goes beyond understanding the words being spoken and delves into the emotions behind those words. When one listens with empathy, they strive to see the world through their partner's eyes, fostering a deeper connection.

Empathy has two primary forms: cognitive and emotional. Cognitive empathy focuses on understanding another's perspective, while emotional empathy feels what the other person is feeling. In intimate conversations, a balance of both forms of empathy is crucial. For example, if a partner shares their frustrations about work, cognitive empathy identifies that frustration while emotional empathy allows for sharing in that discomfort, validating the partner's feelings.

Building empathy within listening transforms conversations, allowing partners to feel seen and understood. This mutual understanding stimulates deeper emotional and sexual intimacy, as each partner recognizes the other's vulnerabilities and desires.

Barriers to Empathy

Even with the best intentions, barriers can impede the practice of empathetic listening:

1. Internal Distractions: Worries, stress, or preoccupations can pull one's focus away from the conversation. This often

leads to half-hearted engagement and can leave one or both partners feeling unheard.

2. Assumptions: Jumping to conclusions about what a partner might say or feel stunts the ability to listen effectively. This lack of open-mindedness can lead to defensive communication instead of collaborative dialogue.

3. Ego: Focusing too much on one's response instead of the other's message can create an imbalance in communication. This egocentric listening can halt the flow of genuine connection.

4. Lack of Knowledge: Sometimes, individuals may feel uncomfortable voicing their feelings, especially if they feel like the partner lacks an understanding of what they are going through. This can create a barrier where one party feels hesitant to share deeply to avoid being misunderstood.

Recognizing and addressing these barriers is essential for cultivating an empathetic listening environment.

Practical Exercises for Active Listening and Empathy

Intentional practice can help develop active listening skills and empathy in relationships. Here are exercises designed to enhance these vital communication tools in intimate conversations:

Exercise 1: The 10-Minute Rule

Dedicate 10 minutes during a quiet time each week for a focused listening session. One partner speaks uninterrupted while the other listens actively. After ten minutes, switch roles. During this time, the listener should practice reflecting, clarifying, and validating emotions. After each session, discuss what felt good and what was challenging. This exercise emphasizes the importance of mindfulness in conversations and helps build a habit of attentive listening.

Exercise 2: Emotion Sharing

Choose a time when both partners are calm to share feelings about a specific topic, such as recent life changes or relationship aspirations. Each partner takes a turn speaking and listening, ensuring to express and acknowledge emotions. Incorporate specific empathetic statements like, "I can see how that would make you feel..." or "That sounds very challenging for you." This practice enhances emotional resonance and understanding between partners.

Exercise 3: Emotion Wheel

Using an emotion wheel, discuss feelings relevant to specific situations. This activity helps partner open up more emotionally. As one partner shares, the listener can identify emotions on the wheel that resonate and affirm those feelings. It encourages vulnerability and acknowledgment of deeper emotional states, supporting an empathetic dialogue.

Exercise 4: Role-Playing

Engage in role-playing exercises where partners assume each other's identities. Each partner articulates feelings and thoughts from the other's perspective. This perspective-shifting exercise enhances cognitive empathy, as partners must articulate a view that may differ from their own.

Exercise 5: Feedback Loop

After any crucial conversation, create a feedback loop. Set aside time to discuss what aspects of the conversation facilitated connection and what could be improved. This practice fostersmgrowth and development in communication skills and builds trust in the relationship.

Strengthening Intimacy Through Listening

As partners engage in empathetic listening, they foster a culture of safety and vulnerability in the relationship. The simple act of truly hearing one another can dissolve walls of misunderstanding and resentment. This process not only enhances emotional intimacy but translates into a more profound sexual connection as well.

When partners feel heard, they are more likely to share openly about their desires, needs, and concerns in both emotional and sexual contexts. In turn, this openness invites further engagement, allowing the cycle of intimacy to grow.

Recognizing the Journey Ahead

The journey of developing active listening skills and empathy is ongoing. It requires patience, practice, and a willingness to be vulnerable. It's essential for couples to remind themselves that setbacks may occur. Difficult conversations about intimacy and feelings may not always yield perfect results, but the commitment to understanding one another remains paramount.

As couples navigate their shared experiences and emotions, the act of listening with empathy will only enrich their journey towards deeper intimacy. Each conversation serves not only as a step towards greater clarity but also deepens the connection between partners, fostering a love that is both resilient and profound.

Continuously nurture this skill, and let it become a vital part of your relationship's fabric. Doing so will undoubtedly lead to a richer, more fulfilling journey together, facilitating not just communication, but a true sharing of lives in their entirety.

Navigating Difficult Conversations

Navigating through the complexities of intimacy can often feel like traversing a labyrinth full of uncertainties, fears, and unspoken needs. For couples striving to deepen their connection, discussing sensitive topics surrounding intimacy can be a daunting challenge. Yet, open communication is paramount for nurturing trust and enhancing emotional and physical closeness. In this subchapter, we explore effective strategies and thoughtful practices for engaging in difficult conversations, equipping couples with the tools needed to navigate these vital discussions with compassion and understanding.

To begin, it is essential to recognize that difficulties often arise from a place of vulnerability. Couplesmay fear judgment, misunderstandings, or even a potential fallout from the conversation. However, it is this very vulnerability that lays the foundation for deep emotional connection. Engaging in difficult dialogues can lead to mutual growth; as partners learn to voice their feelings, needs, and desires, both strengthen the bond that holds them together.

Understanding the Importance of Difficult Conversations

Understanding why these conversations matter is the first step. Intimacy thrives on honesty and transparency; thus, discussing challenging subjects enables partners to align their expectations and fosters a sense of safety in the relationship.

The primary purposes of these conversations include:

1. Clarifying Expectations: Couples can articulate their desires and needs, promoting a mutual understanding of each other's experiences and feelings.

2. Identifying Barriers: Conversations can bring to light underlying fears or concerns that affect intimacy, giving partners the opportunity to address them together.

3. Strengthening Emotional Bonds: Honesty can create a deeper emotional connection as partners show vulnerability and courage by sharing their thoughts and feelings.

4. Encouraging Growth: Each conversation is an opportunity to grow together, fostering a culture of compassion, empathy, and respect.

Preparing for the Conversation

Preparation is key to successful conversations. Taking time to reflect individually can help clarify personal feelings and expectations before discussing them with a partner. Here are some strategies to prepare:

— Self-Reflection: Consider what aspects of intimacy are causing discomfort or need to be addressed. Journaling may help in articulating thoughts clearly.

— Define Objectives: Set clear, realistic goals for the conversation. What outcomes do you hope to achieve? This focus will streamline the dialogue and keep it constructive.

— Choose the Right Moment: Timing matters significantly. Select an appropriate time when both partners are receptive and can dedicate attention without distractions.

— Mindset: Approach the conversation with an open mind and a willingness to listen. This sets the tone for a more productive and compassionate exchange.

Engaging in the Conversation

Once both partners have prepared, it's time to dive into the conversation. Here are practical steps to take:

1. Create a Safe Space
   Establishing an environment conducive to open dialogue is crucial. This might mean choosing a comfortable setting away from the hustle and bustle of daily life. Ensure that both partners feel physically and emotionally secure, and consider minimizing distractions. Gentle affirmations, body language, and eye contact can further reinforce a sense of safety.

2. Use "I" Statements
   Using "I" statements can help in expressing feelings without placing blame. For example, instead of saying, "You

never initiate intimacy," you might say, "I feel neglected when intimacy is one-sided." This approach encourages understanding rather than defensiveness from the partner.

3. Listen Actively
   Active listening involves fully engaging with what the other person is saying. Avoid planning your response while your partner speaks. Instead, show that you are invested in their words through nods, affirmations, and encouraging prompts.

4. Practice Empathy
   Empathy is essential when discussing sensitive subjects. Seek to understand your partner's perspective and feelings. Ask open-ended questions to encourage deeper exploration, such as, "How does that make you feel?" By validating each other's emotions, couples can sometimes diffuse tensions and foster understanding.

5. Role-Playing Scenarios
   Role-playing can be an effective way to prepare for real-life conversations, especially when discussing sensitive topics. Couples can take turns expressing their feelings in a controlled setting while the other practices their responses. Here are a few scenarios:

   - **Scenario 1:** The Desire to Explore New Intimacy Practices
   - Partner A expresses a desire to introduce new elements into their intimate life.
   - Partner B hesitates, feeling nervous about change.
   - Role-play involves Partner A sharing why they feel this exploration could benefit both and Partner B articulating their concerns respectfully.
   - **Scenario 2:** Addressing Decreased Frequency of Intimacy
   - One partner feels that intimacy has dwindled over the months and wants to reopen the conversation surrounding it.

- The role-play focuses on how to express feelings of disconnect without blaming, ensuring both partners feel heard and involved in the solution.
- Scenario 3: Discussing Past Trauma Influence
- A partner wishes to navigate how past experiences affect their current intimacy dynamics.
- Through role-play, this partner expresses their feelings, and the other partner practices active listening, reflecting back what they hear for better understanding.

6. Setting Boundaries and Ground Rules
   To ensure the conversation remains productive, set ground rules such as:

   - No interruptions: Allow each person to finish speaking before responding.
   - No personal attacks: Focus on the issue at hand rather than launching into unrelated grievances.
   - Respectful language: Choose words carefully to avoid angering or provoking defensiveness.

After the Conversation

Post-conversation reflection is just as crucial as the dialogue itself. Consider these steps:

- Check-In: Schedule a follow-up discussion to see how both partners feel after the dialogue, allowing for adjustments and further exploration of unresolved topics.
- Take Action: If both partners agree on changes or growth areas, establish small, achievable steps moving forward.
- Celebrate Progress: Acknowledge and celebrate any improvements or efforts made after the conversation, as this reinforces the positive outcomes of these discussions.

Expert Insights on Difficult Conversations

Experts in relationship counseling emphasize the necessity of compassion during sensitive discussions. According to Dr. John Gottman, a leading researcher on relationships, "The ability to communicate effectively sets the foundation for resolving conflicts." Dr. Esther Perel, a prominent psychotherapist, notes, "Desire and intimacy thrive on openness. Emotional transparency is not a choice but a requirement for closeness." Both encourage couples to embrace discomfort, framing it as an essential part of relationship growth.

Conclusion

Navigating difficult conversations surrounding intimacy is a fundamental skill for couples wishing to enhance their connection. The fears and hesitations that accompany these discussions can be overwhelming, yet the bonds forged through compassion, vulnerability, and understanding are invaluable. Every couple will face challenges, but those who approach each other with open hearts and minds can truly redefine their intimacy. By practicing active listening, utilizing role-play, and establishing safe boundaries, partners can foster deeper emotional connections that extend far beyond the bedroom. Through commitment and cooperation, couples can turn these challenging dialogues into opportunities for healing and growth, ultimately leading to a more satisfying and intimate relationship.

Chapter 4

VULNERABILITY:
THE KEY TO INTIMACY

VULNERABILITY: THE KEY TO INTIMACY

The Power of Vulnerability

Vulnerability is a concept that resonates deeply within the fabric of human relationships. It is often perceived as a weakness, a chink in one's emotional armor. Yet, in the realm of intimacy, vulnerability holds transformative power. When we allow ourselves to be seen, to expose our true selves—flaws, fears, and insecurities—we create a pathway for connection that is unparalleled. This power of vulnerability, when embraced, can strengthen the bonds between partners, creating a richer, more fulfilling relationship.

At its core, vulnerability is about being authentic. It's about shedding the layers we put on for the outside world and revealing the person beneath. In doing so, we invite our partner into our inner sanctum. This requires a leap of faith—one that many couples must navigate together. Many fear that revealing their true selves may lead to rejection, judgment, or loss. However, history has shown us through countless relationships that true intimacy blooms only when both partners feel safe enough to be vulnerable.

Consider the story of Emily and Jake, a couple who had been married for over a decade. On the surface, they appeared to be a model couple—balancing work, family, and social commitments with relative ease. However, beneath that polished facade lay a growing distance that neither was quite able to articulate. They had settled into routines that, while comfortable, lacked the spark of true intimacy.

During a particularly quiet evening, Jake broached the subject. "I feel like we've stopped sharing parts of ourselves with each other," he admitted, his voice tinged with uncertainty. Emily nodded, her heart racing; she felt the same but had been too afraid to voice it. That conversation became a pivotal moment.

Instead of shying away from the discomfort, they embraced their vulnerability. They began to share not just their dreams but their fears, disappointments, and regrets. Emily, in one of their candid conversations, shared how she felt inadequate in both her career and parenting. Jake, in turn, opened up about his struggles with anxiety and how it affected his ability to engage with his family fully. As they shared their perceived weaknesses, they also discovered strengths in one another.

This exchange ignited a profound shift in their relationship. The weight of unspoken words lifted, replaced by a newfound empathy and understanding. No longer were they just partners managing life's logistics; they became co-authors of their emotional story. Their vulnerability created a safe space where they could explore deeper emotional territories without fear of judgment. They realized that true love is not in perfection, but in the acceptance of imperfections.

Through their journey, Emily and Jake learned that being vulnerable also meant allowing themselves to be seen in their entirety. This included their desires and aspirations, which often lay dormant under layers of self-doubt. Opening up to one another was not merely an emotional exercise; it facilitated a greater sexual intimacy that had been lacking in their union.

As they delved deeper into their vulnerable selves, their physical connection flourished as well. They became more in tune with each other's needs, both emotional and physical. This newfound intimacy fostered a deeper understanding of what they desired from one another, enhancing their shared experiences in the bedroom.

Emotionally, Jake found himself more able to voice what he wanted from Emily, while Emily felt free to express her own sexual desires without hesitation. This kind of honesty cultivated an environment for sexual exploration that both found exhilarating as they engaged in a dance of consent and openness. They had stripped away the barriers that had clouded their connection—vulnerability was their key.

Navigating this new emotional terrain was not without its challenges. Fear, the ever-present companion in the vulnerability journey, sometimes crept back in. On some occasions, particularly when the discussions turned to past traumas or insecurities that felt too raw, they found themselves hesitating. Yet, what made the difference was their commitment to return to those conversations. They agreed to greet those fears together and work through them side by side.

The couple learned that vulnerability required trust—a trust they had been slowly rebuilding through their shared experiences. Each time they tackled a moment of vulnerability, they laid another brick on the foundation of their intimacy. They realized that trust does not come easily; it's built through consistent honesty and reliability over time.

Vulnerability also ignited compassion within their relationship. As each shared vulnerability was met with empathy, the cycle of connection deepened. The understanding that neither was alone in their uncertainties fostered a sense of unity. Emily and Jake often discussed how comforting it was to not only hear their partner's struggles but to also relate their own, transforming these conversations into a shared experience that drew them closer.

Moreover, the power of vulnerability did not only reside in their intimate conversations; it extended to their parenting. As they learned to embrace vulnerability as a couple, they began to foster a similar environment with their children. They encouraged their kids to express feelings of fear and disappointment without fear of retribution, promoting an emotional literacy that resonated within the family.

One evening, during a family discussion about school challenges, their son, Liam, hesitantly shared his fear of not being accepted by his peers. For Jake and Emily, this was a pivotal moment—a chance to model vulnerability in action. They shared their own experiences of feeling out of place, validating his feelings and reassuring him that it was okay to feel unsure at times. Liam realized that it was safe to share his vulnerabilities, reinforcing the intimacy within the family unit.

As the journey of vulnerability unfolded for Emily and Jake, they recognized that it was not a one-time event but a continuous practice. Every day presented opportunities to deepen their connection through honesty, encouraging open dialogue about their feelings, desires, and fears. They established weekly check-ins, where they could discuss what was on their hearts without distractions. These sessions became a cherished ritual, allowing them to strengthen the trust they had cultivated.

Through their experiences, Emily and Jake learned that vulnerability is a strength, not a weakness. They discovered that the moments they felt the most exposed often led to the greatest feelings of closeness. It became clear, too, that vulnerability is inherently tied to emotional regulation; by allowing their partner to see their lighter and darker sides, they also became more adept at managing their emotional states together, ultimately making them more resilient.

Consider another couple, David and Sarah, who also journeyed down the path of vulnerability. Their relationship had begun to stagnate, and although they maintained appearances of a happy marriage, both felt disconnected. During a workshop on emotional intimacy, they were introduced to concepts of vulnerability. Initially hesitant, they slowly began to explore this new dimension of their relationship.

David shared how he tended to retreat into silence during conflict rather than expressing his feelings. This vulnerability led to an emotional breakthrough for Sarah, who had often felt frustrated and ignored during these periods. Instead of dismissing his quietness, she committed to encouraging him to open up.

Together, they navigated uncomfortable conversations. David learned to articulate his feelings instead of withdrawing, while Sarah practiced patience and understanding when his words came slowly. This mutual vulnerability led to deep conversations about their childhoods, their dreams, and the pressures they faced as a couple. They discovered layers of each other they had never unveiled before.

Sarah particularly appreciated hearing David's fears about not being a good enough husband or father. It showed her that he cared deeply about their family dynamics. This acknowledgment reinforced her commitment to support him and opened the door for her to express her own insecurities about motherhood—something she had struggled with since the birth of their first child. As their vulnerabilities intertwined, they began to function as a united team, supporting each other through apprehensions.

As their conversations deepened, they also found joy in vulnerability beyond emotions; it enhanced their sexual intimacy as well. Since they had established a safe environment for sharing their feelings, they also started to explore their sexual desires more openly. They became comfortable navigating topics of fantasies and preferences, which only invigorated their physical encounters and attracted them to each other anew.

In sharing intimate details about desires, David and Sarah created new avenues for connection. They began scheduling spontaneous date nights that catered to their mutual interest in adventure. Vulnerability became a bridge they crossed to strengthen their relationship, reshaping the very essence of their connection with one another.

In both Emily and Jake's and David and Sarah's stories, we see that vulnerability is not merely a function of emotional expression; it shapes the foundational dynamics of relationship. Embracing one's true self and allowing a partner to witness one's authenticity paves the way for greater intimacy. It is not enough to simply acknowledge one's vulnerabilities; couples must actively engage them in their relationship journey.

Along the way, it is essential for partners to recognize that vulnerability can sometimes lead to discomfort, and this is natural. The key lies in remaining committed to the process despite the hurdles. Sensitivity may arise, leading to moments of conflict or misunderstanding. However, these moments can prove valuable when handled with care. Navigating discomfort together fosters resilience and trust rather than erodes them.

As we explore deeper connections, we are reminded that vulnerability is a journey, one that can be influenced by past experiences and personal history. Not everyone may be ready to embrace vulnerability at the same pace. For some, these discussions may trigger fears of abandonment or inadequacy based on previous hurts. Partners should be patient and understanding in these instances, working to meet each other where they are.

In essence, vulnerability invites us to experience our relationships authentically—each layer of honesty reveals deeper depths of closeness. As individuals share their emotions without fear of the world's judgments, they foster an environment where true intimacy flourishes. In vulnerable moments, we realize we are not alone; others struggle and triumph alongside us.

Ultimately, as David and Sarah's story demonstrates, the true power of vulnerability lies in its ability to invite connection and understanding. Vulnerability becomes the driving force that leads to emotional healing and intimacy, shaping a narrative woven with shared experiences and mutual respect. The journey may be fraught with challenges, but it is one of the most rewarding experiences that couples can undertake, strengthening their bonds and enhancing their love.

In closing, the next time you face a moment where vulnerability beckons, consider it an opportunity for growth. Embrace your true self, allow your loved one to be a part of the journey, and witness the profound connection that begins to blossom. Remember, vulnerability is the key to unlocking the door to intimacy; it may lead you to the deepest expression of love and connection that you have always been searching for together.

Fears Surrounding Vulnerability

In the journey of intimacy, vulnerability stands as the cornerstone upon which profound connections are built. It is through vulnerability that partners open their hearts and share their true selves, embracing the emotional exposure that comes with deepening their bond. However, alongside this transformative power of vulnerability lies a myriad of fears that can obstruct the path to true intimacy. For many, the prospect of feeling vulnerable can evoke anxiety, discomfort, and even dread. This subchapter delves into the common fears surrounding vulnerability, exploring how these fears can inhibit intimacy, while also providing expert strategies to confront and overcome them.

Understanding the Fears

At the core of vulnerability lies a fear of exposure. Many individuals harbor a deep-seated concern about revealing their true selves, believing that doing so may lead to rejection, judgment, or betrayal. This fear can stem from past experiences, such as childhood trauma, heartbreak in previous relationships, or social conditioning that glorifies stoicism and emotional restraint.

For some, the fear of vulnerability manifests as a reluctance to express emotions openly. They may worry that their feelings will be dismissed or that exposing their inner world will make them appear weak. This notion of weakness is compounded by societal pressures that often equate emotional vulnerability with a lack of strength.

Moreover, the fear of vulnerability can also connect with concerns about self-worth. When individuals do not feel secure in their identities or their value as partners, the thought of being vulnerable can become unbearable. They may ask themselves, "What if I'm not enough?" or, "What if my partner sees my flaws and chooses to leave?" These poignant questions reflect the myriad insecurities that can accompany intimate relationships, often paralyzing individuals from taking the necessary steps toward authentic connection.

Another significant aspect of vulnerability fears is the fear of losing control. For many, vulnerability implies surrendering control, which flies in the face of their desire to maintain a perceived sense of autonomy. This fear can lead to self-protective behaviors, such as building emotional walls, avoiding difficult conversations, or shutting down when faced with intimacy. However, such protective measures can inadvertently create emotional distance between partners, leading to the very outcomes they seek to avoid.

Consequences of Fear

The impact of these fears is profound and multifaceted. When individuals allow their fears surrounding vulnerability to dictate their behavior, they inadvertently create barriers to nurturing intimacy. Emotional closeness requires openness, honesty, and authenticity—all qualities that are inherently stifled when fear takes the reins.

In relationships, fear can manifest in various ways. Partners may withhold affection, refuse to discuss their feelings, or engage in avoidance behaviors to mitigate their discomfort. For example, one partner might notice the other exhibiting signs of emotional withdrawal and may react by becoming distant themselves, creating a vicious cycle that perpetuates disconnection.

Moreover, when fear prevails, partners may resort to defensive communication styles. Instead of expressing their needs or feelings clearly, they may resort to sarcasm, passive-aggressiveness, or outright conflict, all of which detract from the intimacy they so desperately desire. Such patterns not only hinder effective communication but also foster resentment and misunderstanding, creating rifts that can be difficult to bridge.

In the long run, allowing fear to govern one's emotional landscape can contribute to a profound sense of isolation. Individuals may find themselves feeling lonely even when surrounded by their partner, as the barriers erected in the name of self-protection only deepen their sense of disconnect. This emotional isolation can lead to dissatisfaction within the relationship, as the foundational trust and emotional safety required for nurturing intimacy steadily erode.

Confronting Vulnerability Fears

In order to mitigate the destructive effects of vulnerability fears, it is essential for individuals to develop strategies that encourage emotional openness and connection. The following expert strategies can serve as guides for partners seeking to confront their fears surrounding vulnerability and embrace the intimate relationships they desire.

1. Acknowledge Your Fears
   The first step in confronting any fear is to acknowledge its existence. Partners should take time to reflect on their vulnerabilities and identify the specific fears that hold them back from being emotionally open. Journaling, meditative practices, or simply engaging in thoughtful conversations can help clarify these fears. By bringing them to light, individuals can begin to understand the root of their insecurities and the impact they have on their relationship.

2. Communicate Openly
   Once individuals have identified their fears, sharing them with their partner is a crucial next step. Open dialogue about vulnerability fears can foster understanding and compassion, allowing partners to support one another and collectively navigate their emotional landscapes. Partners can create a

safe space where they can openly express their vulnerabilities without fear of judgment. For instance, they might invite each other to share their feelings by saying, "Can we talk about what makes us feel vulnerable in our relationship?"

3. Reframe Vulnerability as Strength
   Reframing vulnerability as an act of strength rather than weakness can significantly shift one's perspective. This involves recognizing that bravery lies in being open and transparent about one's inner world. Couples can engage in exercises that celebrate vulnerability—such as sharing their fears and insecurities while focusing on the strength it takes to do so. This approach can help build a stronger sense of connection as partners learn to appreciate the beauty of emotional exposure.

4. Practice Gradual Exposure
   Facing vulnerability fears can feel overwhelming, but practicing gradual exposure can help ease discomfort. Partners can start with small acts of vulnerability, such as expressing affection through words or sharing thoughts and feelings in low-stakes situations. As they cultivate experiences of emotional openness, they can gradually progress to deeper topics and more significant disclosures. This incremental approach creates a safer environment for intimacy to flourish.

5. Establish Trust
   Building trust is essential in fostering an environment conducive to vulnerability. Couples must work together to create a sense of safety within their relationship. This involves maintaining consistency in words and actions, being trustworthy with shared confidences, and avoiding any form of criticism or judgment. Trust is reinforced through both partners' commitment to honor each other's emotional exposure, thereby allowing them to explore vulnerability without fear of rejection or betrayal.

6. Explore Underlying Issues
    Sometimes, vulnerability fears are symptomatic of deeper issues, such as untreated trauma, attachment insecurities, or low self- esteem. Partners may benefit from engaging in individual or couples therapy, where they can explore the roots of their fears and develop effective coping strategies. A trained therapist can provide valuable tools and insights to help partners navigate these complexities with compassion and support.

7. Embrace Imperfection
    Learning to embrace imperfection is another powerful tool to confront vulnerability fears. No one is perfect, and acknowledging individual flaws, mistakes, and uncertainties can foster a more authentic connection. Couples can practice self-compassion and remind one another that being vulnerable doesn't equate to being flawless. Through shared experiences of imperfection, partners can cultivate a deeper sense of understanding and acceptance between them.

8. Engage in Shared Vulnerable Experiences
    Experiencing vulnerability together can be a transformative journey for couples. Engaging in activities that encourage emotional exposure—such as volunteering for a cause, discussing personal challenges, or participating in creative expression—can help partners bond through shared vulnerability. These experiences can enhance trust and foster intimacy as partners navigate their emotions and fears side-by-side.

9. Focus on the Positive Outcomes
    Finally, reminding oneself of the positive outcomes that can arise from embracing vulnerability can serve as motivation to overcome fears. Couples can journal or discuss instances when vulnerability has led to deeper connections, strengthened trust, or enhanced intimacy in their relationship. Recognizing and celebrating these moments reinforces the notion that vulnerability catalyzes growth, not shame.

Conclusion

The journey toward deeper intimacy is intricately linked to the willingness to embrace vulnerability. While the fears surrounding vulnerability can create daunting obstacles, individuals can confront and mitigate these fears through understanding, communication, reframing, and gradual exposure. Partnering together in this process fosters a sense of safety and, ultimately, strengthens the foundation of their relationship.

As couples learn to navigate their vulnerability fears, they not only enhance their emotional connection but also cultivate a profound understanding of one another, celebrating both their strengths and imperfections. By prioritizing vulnerability and actively working to dismantle the barriers it presents, partners can embark on a journey that culminates in deep intimacy, mutual trust, and an unshakeable bond.

Practicing Vulnerability Together

The foundation of intimacy in any relationship is built on trust and vulnerability. But truly embracing vulnerability can be daunting. It requires individuals to lower their defenses, expose their deepest thoughts, feelings, and insecurities, and place them in front of their partner. This act of opening up is not only a significant step towards deeper connection but also a shared experience that can strengthen the bond between partners. In this subchapter, we will explore various exercises and activities designed to help couples practice vulnerability safely, fostering an environment of openness and trust. To begin, it's essential to create a safe space for vulnerability. Couples should start by discussing what makes them feel secure in their relationship. Each partner ought to express their feelings about sharing personal thoughts and experiences. This conversation is an initial activity that sets the tone for deeper engagement. Consider these questions:

1. What does vulnerability mean to you?
    Through this question, partners can articulate what vulnerability looks like in their eyes. For some, it might mean

sharing secrets or fears, while for others, it could be about expressing the desire for deeper emotional connection.

2. When do you feel most vulnerable?
   Sharing instances when one feels most exposed can shed light on personal insecurities and fears. It helps both partners understand each other's emotional landscapes.

3. What do you need from me to feel safe being vulnerable?**
   This question encourages couples to identify specific actions that can help them feel secure. For example, one partner may need reassurance or may prefer gentle approaches when discussing sensitive topics. It's crucial to communicate these needs clearly to foster a supportive environment.

As partners delve into this discussion, it's important they remain empathetic listeners. Validation of feelings goes a long way in reinforcing that it's safe to be open. Each partner should practice active listening, using techniques such as maintaining eye contact, nodding affirmatively, and paraphrasing what the other says to show understanding.

Once the groundwork is laid, couples can explore specific exercises designed to practice vulnerability together:

1. The Vulnerability Letters:
   Each partner writes a letter revealing their fears, insecurities, or past experiences that still affect them today. They can choose to write about anything that feels significant—insecurities about their bodies, fears of failure, or unresolved traumas. Afterward, couples take turns reading their letters aloud in a quiet, intimate setting. It's vital to approach this exercise without interruption or judgment. After sharing, discuss how those feelings resonate in the present and what they need from each other moving forward.

2. Sharing Personal Stories:
   Think about significant moments in life that shaped who you are today. Each partner should take turns recounting a personal story from their past that they haven't yet shared with their partner. The story could relate to relationships, career struggles, or even childhood memories. This exercise not only opens pathways for vulnerability but also allows partners to see different facets of one another's lives that have contributed to their current selves

3. Fear-Setting Exercise:
   Inspired by Tim Ferriss's concept of fear-setting, this exercise encourages two main activities: identifying fears and understanding their impacts. Each partner lists three fears regarding their relationship or life in general. They then explore the worst-case scenarios that could stem from those fears. Following this, couples articulate what they would do to mitigate those fears or what steps they could take to prevent them from occurring. Discussing these fears and their implications can reveal vulnerabilities and life goals, fostering deeper understanding and intimacy.

4. The Daily Gratitude Exchange:
   Vulnerability also comes from sharing feelingsof appreciation and love. By practicing daily gratitude towards each other, couples can expose their emotional needs and reinforce their bond. Each day, partners should take turns expressing gratitude for the little things that make a difference in their relationship. It could relate to acts of kindness, expressions of love, or even acknowledging moments of shared vulnerability. Over time, this not only deepens connection but encourages partners to view relationship dynamics positively, even when facing challenges.

5. Intimacy Through Art:
   Engaging in art can catalyze vulnerability for many. Couples can create a shared art project that embodies their emotions

and experiences. Whether painting, sculpting, or crafting, while working together, couples can share their thoughts and feelings about their creations. The artwork becomes a tangible representation of vulnerability and a safe outlet for shared expression, leading to discussions around emotions depicted.

6. Physical Vulnerability:
    Physical vulnerability can be an incredibly powerful way to foster emotional closeness. This activity encourages partners to explore touch and physical connection beyond the sexual context. They can dance together, practice yoga, or even engage in a massage session. While one partner takes the lead in being physically vulnerable, the other can practice active listening and emotional presence. Afterward, they can discuss how the physical experience impacted their emotional state and feelings of vulnerability.

7. Creating a Safe Word:
    Introducing a safe word can promote both physical and emotional vulnerability. Couples can choose a word that signifies the need to pause during an emotional conversation if it becomes too overwhelming. This agreement allows for open yet safe dialogues without fear of pushing limits. It reinforces trust and emphasizes that it's okay to express discomfort or the need for space during vulnerable moments.

8. Role Reversal Exercises:
    Engaging in role reversal can enhance empathy and understanding between partners. They can swap roles during discussions, where each partner must argue from the other's perspective. This exercise allows individuals to embody their partner's feelings, and motivations, and decisions. It often leads to revelations about how each partner perceives vulnerability and what emotional triggers exist within the relationship.

9. Building a Shared Vision Board:
   Creating a joint vision board can serve as a platform for vulnerability by encouraging partners to articulate their dreams and intentions for their relationship. Gather materials—magazines, colored papers, or digital imagery—and spend an evening discussing hopes for the future. As you piece together images and words that resonate, couples expose their desires and aspirations, leading to discussions that draw out vulnerabilities tied to their expectations for themselves and the relationship.

10. The Time Capsule:
    Another unique idea is creating a time capsule. Couples can sit together and write down their thoughts, feelings, and shared experiences they'd like to reflect upon in the future. Include reminders of the feelings shared during this moment of vulnerability. Close the capsule and decide when to open it—perhaps on a significant anniversary. Not only does this act promote vulnerability in the present, but it offers a chance for partners to reflect on their journey together later.

11. The Compliment Circle:
    This exercise involves sitting face-to-face and taking turns giving each other compliments. These compliments should be sincere and specific, going beyond mere physical traits. For instance, partners might compliment aspects of personality, strengths they admire, or moments when they have felt particularly loved. The goal is to communicate vulnerability via appreciation and affirmations that nurture both partners' emotional safety.

12. Setting Intentions Together:
    This closing exercise invites partners to connect on an intentional level. Together, discuss goals and intentions for the next month or year, focusing on areas where they hope to practice vulnerability. Whether it's being more open in discussions about insecurities, taking time to explore

intimacy, or sharing personal experiences, creating a shared commitment enhances accountability. This exercise fosters a mindset that values vulnerability as an ongoing practice rather than a one-time activity.

Each of these exercises serves a dual purpose: not only do they promote vulnerability, but they also cultivate greater emotional intimacy. The key to this process is ongoing engagement; couples should consistently check in with one another about their feelings surrounding the exercises they've completed.

After each exercise, partners must reflect on their feelings—what was uncomfortable, what felt good, and what surprised them. As they engage in dialogues about their experiences, they reinforce their emotional connection. Encourage open dialogue using prompts like:

- How did this exercise challenge your understanding of vulnerability?

- What feelings or thoughts surfaced during the activity?

- In what ways do you think this exercise has brought us closer?

This reflective practice ensures that vulnerability becomes an ongoing dialogue rather than a singular moment of sharing.

As couples embark on this journey of shared vulnerability, it is imperative that they remain patient with one another. Opening up takes time, and learning to feel safe in vulnerability is a process. Each partner should also remember that it's normal for discomfort to arise. Instead of shying away from those feelings, use opportunities to explore them together.

Moreover, it's crucial to respect each other's boundaries throughout this journey. If a partner expresses discomfort during an exercise or conversation, the other should honor that boundary without judgment. This respect underscores the foundation of trust necessary for vulnerability to thrive.

Ultimately, practicing vulnerability together is not merely about sharing sharable moments but rather about becoming attuned to each other in a deeper, more profound way. It fosters a relationship characterized by open communication, trust, and unwavering support. Over time, participating in these exercises and experiences will help partners cultivate an intimacy that rises above the surface, delving into the very heart of their emotional connections.

As couples navigate the complexities of vulnerability, they may find that their intimate relationship flourishes when both partners feel safe, seen, and appreciated for who they are. The journey of practicing vulnerability together is a lifelong commitment, one that brings tremendous rewards inthe form of lasting love, understanding, and connection.

—— Chapter 5 ——

THE DANCE OF DESIRE

THE DANCE OF DESIRE

Evolving Desires

As relationships evolve, so too do the sexual attractions and desires that make them unique. The initial spark that ignites passion can morph into something deeper, richer, and, at times, more complex. Couples often find themselves navigating this landscape of shifting desires, and understanding these changes is crucial to maintaining intimacy. In this subchapter, we explore the evolution of sexual attraction within long-term relationships, incorporating personal stories from couples and expert insights to illuminate the journey.

The journey of desire in a relationship often begins with an intense attraction. This initial phase is characterized by excitement, curiosity, and an almost magnetic pull towards one another. Couples frequently describe this period as exhilarating, filled with moments of discovery and a newfound sense of self-awareness. For John and Lisa, the thrill of their early relationship remains an indelible memory, even as they've grown together over the years.

"In the beginning, it was all about the rush, the excitement of being together," John recalls. "We were constantly discovering each other, whether it was through late-night conversations or spontaneous adventures. I remember the first time we kissed—everything around us faded away, and it was just us. That feeling of wanting to be close to her was all-consuming."

Lisa adds, "It felt like a movie. There was this chemistry that pulled us together. We were both so in tune with each other's bodies, and everything was charged with electricity. That initial infatuation was exhilarating, but I think we started to realize that desire would evolve as time went on."

As relationships progress, the intensity of that initial attraction can naturally wane. Routine, life stresses, and the familiarity that comes with long-term commitment can dull the edges of desire. This doesn't imply a loss of love or attraction; rather, it signals a shift toward a deeper connection rooted in emotional intimacy.

This transition can be challenging for many couples. Often, partners find themselves questioning whether their desire for each other is as strong as it once was. Dr. Susan Hardwick, a noted relationship therapist, emphasizes that this phase doesn't warrant concern but rather a reassessment of how desire manifests in a committed relationship. "The evolution of desire is a natural part of any long-term relationship," she explains. "It's about learning to embrace the ebb and flow of attraction and finding new ways to connect with one another."

A crucial aspect of navigating changing desires is communication. While it may seem daunting, openly discussing how sexual attraction is evolving can foster understanding and intimacy. Sarah and David experienced a period where they struggled to connect sexually, leading to feelings of frustration on both sides. Recognizing the need for honest dialogue, they made it a priority to share their feelings.

Sarah reflects on this turning point: "We were both feeling distant and frustrated, but we hadn't talked about it. It was during a weekend getaway that we finally sat down and had a heart-to-heart. I shared how I felt like our sex life had become routine, and he admitted that he felt the same. It felt like a weight lifted off my shoulders just to know we were in the same boat."

David interjects, "Once we opened up about it, things started to shift. We realized that our problem wasn't a lack of attraction; it was more about how we were connecting in that area. From then on, we made it a point to explore our desires without judgment."

Expert tips on embracing these conversations include setting aside a time when both partners can open up without pressure. It's essential to create a safe space where both individuals feel valued and respected. In doing so, couples can rediscover their physical connection and rebuild their desire. For Sarah and David, this effort led to a rekindled passion as they explored new ways of connecting intimately.

As partners grow, their interests, values, and goals may change, and this evolution directly impacts sexual desires. Jessica and Tom found their relationship entering a new phase after becoming parents. The demands of parenting shifted their focus away from their sexual relationship, leading to feelings of disconnect.

"After we had our first child, it felt like all of our energy was directed towards the baby," Jessica explains. "We were exhausted most days and had little time to focus on each other. Our sexual relationship took a back seat, and I struggled with that for a long time."

Tom shares, "I absolutely felt that shift too. I wanted to be there for Jessica and support her, but I also missed our intimacy. I had to constantly remind myself that we were still a couple despite being parents."

Recognizing the need for intimacy amidst the chaos of parenting, they began scheduling regular date nights, where they could reconnect outside of their roles as parents. This time apart from parental obligations allowed them to nurture their bond and explore their desires in a relaxed setting. It was during one of these dates that Tom surprised Jessica by discussing how they both could engage in new experiences together.

"We started talking about things we wanted to explore—both in and out of the bedroom," he recalls. "This openness helped me realize that intimacy didn't have to look the same as when we were child-free. It could adapt, and we had the power to shape it together."

Many couples find that exploring new activities or experiences together can reignite desire. Whether it's taking a dance class, trying out new hobbies together, or even planning a spontaneous weekend getaway, these shared experiences can stimulate emotional and physical intimacy. Dr. Emily Langston, a marriage and family therapist, emphasizes that novelty is a significant factor in sustaining desire. "When couples engage in new and exciting activities, it creates fresh dopamine responses in the brain, which enhances attraction," she explains. "It's essential for couples to find ways to inject novelty and excitement into their relationship, especially as years go by and the initial spark begins to fade."

Anecdotal evidence from couples supports Dr. Langston's advice. For Michelle and Bruce, introducing new experiences into their relationship helped breathe new life into their intimacy. "We decided to take up salsa dancing as a couple—even though we weren't necessarily dancers," Michelle explains with a laugh. "But what I found is that it wasn't just about dancing. It forced us to be physically close, and it reminded us of the fun we shared at the beginning of our relationship."

Bruce agrees, adding, "Getting out there and being silly together really turned the heat up. It turned out to be a great way to explore each other's bodies in a fun, low-pressure context. That sense of lightness and laughter let us relax and reconnect physically and emotionally."

Another important aspect of evolving desires is acknowledging and confronting personal changes that can affect sexual attraction. Life transitions, such as aging, health concerns, and individual self-esteem, may influence an individual's perception of themselves and their desirability. For instance, as her body changed after giving birth, Lauren struggled with feeling attractive to her partner. Her experience mirrors what many women face in similar transitions.

"I went through a really tough time after having kids. My body didn't feel like mine anymore. I didn't want to be intimate because I didn't feel good about the way I looked," she shares.

Jay, her husband, noticed this shift but wasn't sure how to approach the topic. Eventually, he expressed his desire to help her feel more confident. "One night, I just told her that she was beautiful to me, no matter what. I wanted her to see herself as I saw her. But we also talked about her feelings, allowing her to express her discomfort without judgement."

This conversation marked a turning point for Lauren, who began to embrace self-acceptance and gradually sought to share her journey with Jay. "It was a relief to have that conversation.

We started exploring our intimacy in a new way, focusing on what felt good, rather than how I felt about my body."

Self-acceptance, as Lauren discovered, is often the key to restoring desire. Moreover, experts recommend that partners offer each other emotional support and encouragement, reinforcing their bond despite any changes they may face. This support not only aids in sustaining desire but also strengthens emotional intimacy, allowing partners to navigate the ups and downs of their evolving relationship together.

Embracing evolving desires also means recognizing the influence of external factors on intimacy. Stress from work, family responsibilities, or financial concerns can take a toll on sexual attraction. Discovery through shared experiences can help couples adeptly manage these factors without compromising their connection.

Andrew and Kate, who have been married for over a decade, illustrate how outside pressures can affect desire yet also provide opportunities for growth. "We went through a rough patch when work demands became overwhelming for both of us," Andrew explains. "I found myself preoccupied with deadlines and was hardly present for Kate, which made me miss our intimate moments more than ever."

Kate recalls, "I felt left out of Andrew's world and was frustrated because I felt neglected. We had to have another honest talk about how we were both feeling, and that led us to prioritize time for each other, despite the chaos. We established a no-phone zone during dinner, and that little boundary made a huge difference in reconnecting."

From that point on, both Andrew and Kate committed to being more intentional about how they interacted with each other during stressful times. Although there were still challenges to face, they found that taking time to focus on each other helped maintain their connection and rekindle desire.

As relationships progress, sexual attraction fluctuates due to various emotional, physical, and external factors. It's natural to encounter peaks and valleys in intimacy throughout a partnership. Recognizing this ebb and flow is vital—what worked once may no longer resonate at different stages in the relationship.

Instead of viewing these changes as a loss, couples can foster a growth mindset, allowing their intimacy to transform through adaptation and exploration. This perspective invites a sense of curiosity and playfulness in navigating evolving desires.

To cultivate this growth, couples are encouraged to engage in activities that invite open-ended exploration of their intimacy. For some couples, this is as simple as taking a weekend for an intimate retreat; for others, it may involve participating in workshops or reading material focused on enhancing intimacy and connection.

Rather than viewing changing desires as obstacles, consider them opportunities for rediscovery. Couples that approach this journey with openness will likely find new pathways to intimacy and connection—from the importance of ongoing communication and self- acceptance to the joyful exploration of new experiences. Every relationship has a uniquely beautiful rhythm, wherein evolving desires can lead to deeper connection, resilience, and ultimately, a more profound love.

To summarize, sexual attraction is not a static entity relegated to the early days of a relationship. It is a dynamic force that reflects both personal changes and relational growth. By embracing open communication, nurturing emotional intimacy, and remaining adaptable, couples can navigate the evolving landscape of desire together. In doing so, they pave the way for a lasting and fulfilling relationship that continually deepens through every phase of life.

Evolving desires are a testament to love's enduring nature, and each shift—whether it comes from within or from external circumstances—can ultimately strengthen the bond between partners. The dance of desire continues, flourishing through shared experiences, understanding, and the commitment to grow together.

Keeping the Spark Alive

In the intricate tapestry of long-term relationships, the initial spark of desire can sometimes fade, buried under the weight of daily responsibilities, routines, and life changes. Yet, with intention and creativity, couples can reignite that passion and keep the flame of desire alive. This subchapter will explore practical tips and innovative ideas designed to help partners maintain their emotional and sexual connection. By incorporating these activities into everyday life, couples can create a vibrant relationship filled with excitement and profound intimacy.

1. Prioritize Regular Date Nights
    One of the simplest yet most effective ways to keep the spark alive is to carve out time specifically dedicated to each other. Regular date nights provide an opportunity for couples to reconnect amidst the chaos of daily life. Prioritizing time together helps reinforce the idea that your relationship is essential.

    Practical Tip: Consider setting a recurring night each week or month, and make it a non-negotiable part of your schedule. Keep the date night fresh by alternating who plans the evening or trying new activities together. Here are some creative date night ideas to explore:

- Theme Nights: Choose a theme—Italian, Mexican, or a favorite movie—and plan an evening around it. Cook a meal, decorate your space, and even dress accordingly.

- Outdoor Adventures: Explore nature by going for a hike, visiting a nearby beach, or having a picnic in the park. Connecting with nature can reinvigorate both your spirits and your relationship.

- Cultural Experiences: Attend a local concert, gallery opening, or theater performance. Engaging with the arts together can inspire deeper conversations and shared experiences. By consistently making time for each other, couples cultivate an atmosphere where romance can flourish.

2. Foster Emotional Intimacy
   While physical connection is crucial, emotional intimacy serves as the foundation for lasting desire. Being open and vulnerable with each other creates a safe space for both partners to express their true feelings, desires, and concerns.

   Practical Tip: Engage in deep conversations without distractions. Set aside time to discuss your dreams, fears, and the things that excite you. Use prompts or questions to guide the conversation, such as:

   - What is something you've always wanted to try together?
   - How can we support each other's personal growth?
   - What are your favorite memories from our time together?

   Ensure that these conversations are balanced, allowing each partner to share without interruption. Listening with empathy reinforces connection, fostering a sense of safety that enhances desire.

3. **Explore Each Other's Love Languages**
Understanding and speaking each other's love language is key in maintaining emotional intimacy. Gary Chapman's concept of love languages—word of affirmation, acts of service, receiving gifts, quality time, and physical touch—highlights how partners may express and receive love differently.

Practical Tip: Take the time to identify your love languages. Discuss them with each other to discover how you can better show affection in ways that resonate. If one partner feels loved through physical touch, prioritize cuddling, holding hands, or gentle kisses throughout the day. If another values acts of service, consider surprising your partner with help around the house or completing a task that they dislike.

By tailoring expressions of love based on each partner's preferences, couples can enhance feelings of connection and, ultimately, desire.

4. **Engage in New Activities**
Novelty plays a significant role in reigniting desire and excitement. Trying new activities together not only breaks the monotonous routine but also encourages partners to work as a team, fostering connection.

Practical Tip: Choose an activity you've both been curious about but haven't yet tried—whether it's salsa dancing, pottery classes, or cooking a new cuisine. The shared experience of learning something new can create a sense of accomplishment and closeness.

Additionally, consider exploring outdoor activities like rock climbing, zip-lining, or canoeing. These activities often generate adrenaline and excitement, amplifying your bond and enhancing attraction. Remember to embrace any imperfections; laughter and support during mishaps can enrich your experience together.

5. Create Rituals and Traditions
    Building rituals or traditions fosters a sense of unity and provides a framework for connection. These shared practices can be simple yet meaningful, marking transitions or special occasions in a way that strengthens the relationship.

    Practical Tip: Designate a weekly or monthly ritual that's unique to you as a couple. This might be:

    −   Sunday Morning Breakfast: Treat it as a special occasion by brewing a pot of coffee, making your favorite meals, and enjoying leisurely conversations together.

    −   Annual Getaway: Choose a destination you both love or explore somewhere new each year. Having that time set aside reinforces your commitment to quality time.

    −   Monthly Love Letters: Take turns writing a letter focused on what you appreciate about one another. Exchange and read them aloud over a dinner date—this can boost emotional intimacy and connection.

    These rituals become a touchstone in your relationship, drawing you back to moments of joy and intimacy.

6. Connect Through Physical Touch
    Physical touch is a crucial element of desire. Ensuring a range of physical contact throughout each day helps strengthen the emotional bond between partners. It's essential not to underestimate the power of simple gestures.

    Practical Tip: Make a conscious effort to touch throughout the day. This can mean holding hands while walking, cuddling on the couch, or stealing kisses in the kitchen. Establishing routines around physical touch, like ending your workday with a warm embrace or having a nightly ritual of snuggling in bed, can enhance both desire and comfort.

7. Communicate About Desires

   Open communication surrounding sexual desires and preferences is essential in keeping passion alive. Partners should feel safe to express what they enjoy, what they might want to try, and to discuss any hesitations or needs they have without fear of judgment.

   Practical Tip: Create a comfortable space for these conversations, free from distractions. Use prompts to guide the dialogue, such as:

   - What does intimacy mean to you?
   - Are there new things that you'd like to explore together sexually?
   - How can we ensure both of our needs are being met?

   Encourage ongoing dialogues rather than one-time discussions. This continual communication nurtures understanding and connection.

8. Infuse Spontaneity

   Predictability can lead to stagnation, so injecting spontaneity into your relationship can reignite passion. Surprise your partner with spontaneous gestures that show your love and desire.

   Practical Tip: Find little ways to surprise each other. This can be as simple as leaving a note in their bag, planning an impromptu picnic, or suggesting a last-minute getaway. Even unexpected compliments or affectionate messages during the day can break the routine and uplift spirit.

   Spontaneity doesn't need to be extravagant; the affection behind the gesture makes it special.

9. Explore Sensory Experiences

   Bringing new sensory experiences into your relationship can drastically enhance intimacy. The human senses create powerful connections, making shared experiences unforgettable.

Practical Tip**: Engage in activities that stimulate the senses:

- Cooking Together: Choose a recipe that incorporates a variety of aromas, colors, and flavors. Cooking together promotes teamwork and offers delicious rewards.

- Massage Exchange: Set up a cozy space with dim lights, soothing music, and oils or lotions. Take turns giving each other sensual massages, which can spark desire and connection.

- Art Activities: Create something together! This can be painting, creating music, or even writing poetry. These activities can invoke laughter and foster artistic collaboration, strengthening your bond.

10. Don't Neglect the Power of Humor
    Laughter is a crucial ingredient in relationships. Humor helps alleviate stress, increases attractiveness, and creates shared joy. Maintaining a lighthearted approach, even in challenging times, can alleviate the pressures of routine or adversity.

    Practical Tip: Incorporate fun and humor into your daily lives. Watch comedies, share funny anecdotes, or create inside jokes. You might even want to try intentional laughter exercises or playful challenges, like a dance-off in the kitchen.

    Through humor, couples can reinforce their connection, making their relationship feel invigorating rather than mundane.

Final Thoughts

Trying to keep the spark alive is not about grand gestures or constant excitement; rather, it's the small, intentional actions that build a sustainable foundation for intimacy. By prioritizing time together, fostering emotional connection, communicating openly, and embracing spontaneity, couples can cultivate an environment ripe for desire.

Relationships are a journey filled with evolving emotional landscapes, and it's crucial to embrace the ups and downs along the way. Every step you take together, every laugh you share, and every heart shared in conversation brings you closer. Keep the dance of desire alive by committing to each other and actively seeking ways to connect beyond the physical, creating a partnership that thrives in love, intimacy, and excitement.

The Impact of Life Changes

Life is a continuous series of transitions, and each transition has the potential to shift the balance of intimacy and desire in a relationship. Whether welcoming a new child into the family, embarking on a new career, or navigating the complexities of aging, these life changes can significantly impact sexual intimacy. Understanding how these external factors can influence your relationship dynamics is crucial for couples who aspire to maintain a vibrant connection. In this subchapter, we will dive into how major life changes can create both challenges and opportunities for intimacy, offering strategies to help couples foster connection during times of adjustment.

Embracing Parenthood

One of the most significant life changes many couples experience is the transition into parenthood. The excitement and joy of welcoming a child can be overwhelming, yet it can also lead to stress and emotional exhaustion. The impending responsibilities of caring for a newborn can shift a couple's focus, often diverting attention away from their relationship and sexual intimacy.

As the arrival of a baby takes center stage, couples may find that their time and energy are allocated primarily to the needs of their child. The demands of caring for an infant—feeding, changing, soothing, and sleepless nights—can lead to feelings of fatigue, consequently causing sexual intimacy to take a back seat. Parents may also face body image issues as they adapt to postpartum changes, and the emotional rollercoaster of parenthood can add pressure and strain to the relationship.

While it's understandable that parental responsibilities take precedence, couples cannot forget the essential aspect of nurturing their relationship. It is vital to make a conscious effort to reconnect physically and emotionally amidst the chaos of parenting. Setting aside time for date nights, whether at home or away, can help rekindle the flame. Consider establishing a routine where both partners exert an effort to prioritize their relationship, even if it means seeking help from family or hiring a babysitter occasionally.

Additionally, openly discussing your feelings about the challenges of parenting can foster emotional intimacy. Sharing experiences, both joyful and challenging, will not only strengthen your bond but also create a supportive environment in which both partners feel seen and valued.

Career Transitions

Similar to the challenges posed by parenthood, major career changes can profoundly impact sexual intimacy. Whether it's a job promotion, a new position, or a shift in responsibilities, the stress and demands of professional life can spill over into personal relationships. The emotional labor associated with navigating a new work environment or maintaining work-life balance can lead to increased stress and, consequently, decreased sexual desire.

The struggle to adapt to new roles may spark feelings of anxiety or insecurity, which can create distance between partners. The pressure to perform at work can lead to late nights, distractions, and a reduced focus on intimate moments. It is crucial to recognize how these shifts in focus can affect both partners and the relationship as a whole.

To address the toll that career transitions can take on intimacy, couples might consider engaging in regular check-ins about their respective workloads and stress levels. Open communication allows partners to express their feelings about their professional lives while fostering a supportive dialogue. Understanding the external pressures each partner faces can ignite empathy and compassion, helping to bridge any emotional gaps.

Prioritize quality time together, even amidst busy schedules. Take intentional breaks throughout the week to connect, whether through shared meals, walks, or simple conversations about your day. Creating rituals of connection, like sharing a bedtime routine, can provide opportunities for intimacy to flourish, even during stressful times.

Navigating Aging

Aging is a natural life transition that can introduce its own set of challenges to sexual intimacy. As individuals age, they may experience changes in physical health, energy levels, and sexual function. These factors can impact desires and lead to feelings of frustration or inadequacy, affecting intimacy between partners.

The societal pressures surrounding aging—such as the perception of a diminished sex drive—can lead to feelings of disappointment and embarrassment about sexual performance. Couples may find themselves grappling with emotional vulnerabilities as they face the realities of aging together.

To maintain intimacy during the aging process, it is essential for partners to communicate openly about their physical and emotional changes. Discussing sexual health openly will help dispel any myths about aging and sexuality. Adjustments may be necessary for sexual activities to accommodate physical changes, but embracing new forms of intimacy can lead to fulfilling experiences. This can range from exploring various forms of touch to engaging in playful activities that foster lightheartedness and connection.

Rituals that promote physical affection—such as massages, cuddling, or simply holding hands—can serve to maintain a sense of closeness.

Acknowledging that intimacy is multifaceted can shift the focus from solely sexual activity to a deeper understanding of each other's needs and desires.

Coping with External Stressors

While parenthood, career changes, and aging are significant transitions, various external stressors can also interfere with intimacy. Financial strains, family conflicts, or health issues may contribute to the stress couples experience. The key is to recognize how these external factors can contribute to emotional distance and impact sexual intimacy.

Creating a supportive environment in which both partners can share their challenges is vital for fostering intimacy. Encourage open dialogue about the external pressures affecting the relationship, and make an effort to support each other. Sharing burdens and seeking solutions together cultivates a sense of teamwork and connection.

Couples may find that rediscovering shared hobbies or engaging in activities that bring joy can help alleviate some stress. Laughter and shared experiences can serve as antidotes to stress, providing opportunities for couples to reconnect emotionally. Finding activities that both partners enjoy, whether cooking together, taking walks, or exploring new hobbies, can help build resilience amid stress.

Intentional Intimacy Practices

Integrating practices that foster intimacy into daily routines can create a solid foundation for couples navigating change. Here are several strategies designed to help couples maintain connection during challenging life transitions:

1. Prioritize Emotional Check-Ins: Set a regular time to discuss feelings, updates, and challenges. Forming a habit of emotional check-ins helps in staying connected, allowing partners to share vulnerabilities without judgment.

2. Schedule Regular Date Nights: Make it a point to have regular date nights or dedicated time for each other. Prioritizing this will show both partners the importance of keeping their connection alive.

3. Explore new forms of intimacy: Sometimes, exploring new forms of intimacy can include anything from creating new sexual experiences and scenarios to engaging in discussions about fantasies or desires. This exploration can reduce performance pressure and reignite excitement.

4. Practice Gratitude: Expressing gratitude for one another can bolster emotional intimacy. Regularly acknowledging each other's contributions, both big and small, can shift the focus towards appreciation and create a nurturing environment.

5. Incorporate Mindfulness Practices: Engage in mindfulness together, whether through meditation, yoga, or simply enjoying quiet time together. This practice can help cultivate a sense of connection and presence in each moment.

6. Communicate Needs Clearly: Encourage open dialogue about sexual needs and preferences. Establishing a safe space for discussing these subjects helps clear up misunderstandings and fosters emotional intimacy.

7. Embrace Flexibility: As life changes occur, remaining flexible and adaptable can alleviate pressure. Embrace the idea that intimacy can take various forms. Allow the needs and desires of both partners to evolve, rather than fixating on a singular definition of intimacy.

8. Celebrate Progress: Acknowledge progress as a couple, no matter how small. Celebrating milestones in intimacy—such as communicating openly, spending quality time, or engaging in new experiences—can reinforce connection and motivation.

9. Seek Professional Support: If navigating life changes proves overwhelming, consider seeking the support of a professional therapist or counselor. A neutral third party can facilitate communication and help couples identify underlying issues affecting intimacy.

In Summary

Life changes are a natural and inevitable part of the human experience, and couples must be equipped to navigate these challenges together. Parenthood, career transitions, and aging can all impact intimacy, but they also offer opportunities for growth and deeper connection. By fostering open communication, practicing resilience, and prioritizing intentional intimacy, couples can weather the storms of life while keeping their relationship vibrant and fulfilling. Adapting to these changes isn't always easy, but with perseverance and mutual support, partners can discover new dimensions of love, desire, and intimacy along the way.

Ultimately, remember that the journey through these transitions is something that couples navigate together—fostering unity, resilience, and a profound appreciation for each other amid life's beautiful complexities.

Chapter 6

INTIMACY BEYOND THE BEDROOM

INTIMACY BEYOND THE BEDROOM

Building Emotional Closeness

In relationships, the fabric of intimacy is woven through many threads, and among the most crucial is emotional closeness. This depth of connection fosters feelings of love, trust, and understanding, serving as the bedrock upon which sexual intimacy rests. Couples often find that their emotional bonding is what truly enriches their experiences together, making them feel not just physically connected, but deeply understood and valued. Consequently, cultivating this emotional closeness becomes paramount for creating an enduring and fulfilling relationship.

Understanding emotional closeness begins with recognizing that intimacy extends beyond the bedroom. Although sexual intimacy can be a significant aspect of a romantic relationship, it is essential to acknowledge that emotional bonding lays the groundwork for a deeper sexual connection. Emotional closeness can manifest through shared experiences, open communication, and the mutual vulnerability that partners exhibit towards one another.

One of the first steps to building emotional closeness is actively engaging in shared experiences. These experiences can serve to unite couples on a deeper level. Whether through taking a cooking class together, embarking on a weekend getaway, or even tackling a home improvement project, shared activities allow partners to invest in quality time. Such quality engagements provide the setting for partners to connect outside the traditional realms of their day-to-day life.

Consider Jack and Lila, a couple who found that the monotony of their routine had created a distance between them. They initiated a weekly date night, exploring new restaurants in their city or attending local art shows. During these outings, they found themselves talking more freely and openly than they had in months. Each week, they looked forward to sharing experiences that allowed them a glimpse into each other's passions and interests.

Their newfound energy brought excitement back into their relationship, nurturing emotional closeness that translated into deeper physical intimacy. Communication plays a pivotal role in forging emotional bonds. Formanycouples, however, communicating effectively can be a challenge. The art of communication involves not just speaking your mind but actively listening to your partner, validating their feelings, and fostering an environment where both parties feel heard and understood. When couples engage in open and honest discussions, they pave the way for a more enriching relationship.

To foster emotional vulnerability, partners need to feel safe and secure in their communication. They must create a climate in which each partner can express their thoughts, emotions, and fears without judgment. A key strategy is practicing active listening: focusing entirely on the speaker, providing feedback, and reframing what has been said to ensure understanding. For example, instead of interrupting your partner to offer solutions, validate their feelings first by saying, "I can see how that situation would be upsetting for you." Such validations not only affirm your partner's emotions but also create pathways for deeper conversations.

Emily and Jacob exemplify how conversation can deepen emotional intimacy. Early in their relationship, they struggled with misunderstandings and assumptions. It wasn't until they adopted the practice of sharing their day—what went well, what frustrated them, and what they were looking forward to—that they realized the power of open dialogue. This simple ritual evolved into a significant tradition for them. They began to share not only their day-to-day lives but also their fears, dreams, and aspirations.

Through these conversations, Emily and Jacob learned about each other's backgrounds, priorities, and unmet emotional needs. Each partner began to understand the motivations behind the other's actions more deeply. As a result, they became increasingly attuned to one another's emotional landscapes, a foundation that significantly enhanced their sexual intimacy.

However, emotional closeness does not occur overnight. It requires patience, dedication, and intentionality. It often takes a mutual commitment from both partners to invest in the practice of vulnerability and openness. One practical approach is to incorporate vulnerability exercises into daily life. For instance, couples might dedicate a day each week to discussing deeper topics, or even utilize prompts to guide their conversations.

One such exercise involves defining each partner's emotional needs. Each person can list their top three needs in the relationship and share them with the other. This exercise encourages honesty and fosters understanding. By clearly expressing their emotional needs, each partner creates an opportunity for the other to acknowledge and validate those needs, reinforcing the bond between them.

Additionally, building emotional closeness also involves engaging in moments of affection beyond sexual expression. Simple acts of kindness and connection—such as holding hands during a walk, hugging after a long day, or sharing a cup of tea—can have profound impacts on how partners perceive and feel about each other. These small gestures often signal a deep commitment and affection, helping to establish an emotional connection that underscores the relationship.

Consider Mia and Scott, who actively incorporated nurturing gestures into their daily routines. Despite their busy lives, they made a conscious effort to reconnect before bed each night. Their routine included sharing what they were grateful for that day and offering each other a few gentle compliments. This practice not only enhanced their emotional bond but also encouraged them to appreciate one another in ways they hadn't previously. As their emotional intimacy grew, they found that their sexual closeness naturally deepened as well.

Another critical aspect of building emotional closeness is self-awareness and personal growth. When partners dedicate themselves to understanding their emotions, triggers, and patterns, they can communicate more effectively with their significant other. Self-awareness allows individuals to engage with their partners from a place of understanding rather than defensiveness.

For some couples, journaling can be a beneficial tool for enhancing self-awareness. Reflecting daily on emotions and experiences can clarify what each partner might want to express during their discussions. By acknowledging their feelings on paper, partners prepare themselves for more meaningful conversations when they engage with one another.

Incorporating rituals into the relationship can also strengthen the emotional bond. These rituals can range from monthly check-ins, where partners discuss their emotional states and relationship goals, to yearly traditions that celebrate their commitment to one another. Rituals create a sense of stability and predictability, allowing partners to feel secure in expressing their emotions and needs.

Furthermore, shared responsibilities can unify couples by fostering emotional support. Engaging in tasks together helps partners feel they are working as a team, reinforcing their connection. Collaborative chores, such as cooking, cleaning, or planning a family event, strengthen the partnership while distributing the emotional load that often arises within relationships.

Lastly, it is crucial for partners to cultivate a sense of gratitude and appreciation for one another. Expressing appreciation on a regular basis serves to validate the partner's efforts and experiences within the relationship. Encouraging words can alter emotional atmospheres, allowing partners to feel special and cherished, effectively enhancing their emotional bond.

In sum, the journey to emotional closeness is an ongoing commitment that requires consistent effort from both partners. The path is distinct for every couple, shaped by their unique histories, experiences, and love languages. Shared experiences, open dialogue, and small gestures of affection all contribute to a profound emotional connection that acts as a sturdy foundation for a fulfilling romantic relationship.

As intimacy expands beyond mere physicality, partners can recognize and appreciate the complexities of emotional bonding. By nurturing emotional closeness, couples can unlock a deeper level of understanding and satisfaction in their relationships, ultimately cultivating an enriching environment where both partners feel cherished, respected, and deeply connected.

Activities that Foster Connection

In the journey of nurturing intimacy beyond the physical realm, couples discover thatthe bonds of connectioncan be forged througha multitude of shared experiences and activities. While sexual intimacy holds its own significance, emotional intimacy often flourishes in the spaces where partners engage in non-sexual endeavors that allow them to explore each other's hearts and minds. This subchapter will delve into a variety of activities that couples can partake in together, each designed to strengthen their emotional bond while promoting a deeper understanding of one another.

One of the most effective ways to foster emotional intimacy is through shared hobbies. Identifying and pursuing interests that resonate with both partners offers a wonderful opportunity to collaborate, communicate, and grow together. Whether it's cooking, gardening, or learning a new craft, these activities can transform mundane moments into cherished memories.

Cooking together can be a fun and rewarding experience. The kitchen becomes a canvas for creativity, where partners can express themselves through culinary art. Try exploring different cuisines; perhaps dedicate a weekend to preparing dishes from a country you both dream of visiting. As you chop, sauté, and taste together, you engage in conversation about flavors, cultures, and traditions. Cooking is inherently collaborative, which necessitates communication and teamwork, creating a shared purpose and reinforcing your partnership bonds. Moreover, the shared success of a well-prepared meal can lead to feelings of accomplishment and joy, deepening your overall connection.

Gardening, on the other hand, presents a unique opportunity to even further bond through a shared investment in life. Planting flowers, vegetables, or herbs creates a physical representation of your unity that flourishes together. As you gather supplies, prepare the soil, and plant the seeds, you are also nurturing each other's dreams and hopes. Over time, watching your garden grow can symbolize the growth of your relationship. This nature-infused activity encourages you to communicate about care routines, and the joys of harvest lead to celebrations, whether small or grand. Gardening can also provide a peaceful environment for intimate conversations, allowing partners to connect on deeper levels amidst the tranquility.

Artistic endeavors often inspire emotional growth and connection. Engaging in activities like painting, drawing, or pottery can be a powerful vehicle for expressing emotions that may be hard to verbalize. Attending an art class together can ignite creativity and encourage playfulness within the relationship. The act of creating side by side provides not just a moment to bond over the creative process, but allows for natural conversations to flow about individual perspectives, inspirations, and artistic intentions. Supporting and encouraging each other during this process not only strengthens your connection but can also enhance your appreciation for each other's unique identities.

Exploring the outdoors together can lead to profound shared experiences that cultivate emotional intimacy. Whether it's hiking, biking, or simply taking a walk in the park, being in nature invokes a sense of peace and connectedness—both to the world around you and to each other. Choose scenic trails or visit local parks that encourage exploration not only of the landscape but also of each other. As you share stories of your past, discuss your future aspirations, or simply enjoy the rhythm of your footsteps together, these moments infused with the beauty of nature can solidify your emotional bond.

Incorporating regular date nights, whether in or out of the house, can significantly enhance your connection. Transition these outings from mere romantic dinners into opportunities for shared experiences that go beyond the superficial elements. Attend workshops or classes together that cover a wide range of themes—cooking, dance, music, or even volunteering. Each shared experience amplifies the laughter, connection, and memories within your relationship. It is a time dedicated to discovering new aspects of each other's personalities in a relaxed and fun environment. Make it an adventure to try something none of you has done before, ensuring it's a joint exploration.

Volunteering together can foster a profound sense of connection as you share the experience of being a part of something greater than yourselves. Choosing a cause that resonates with both partners allows for deeper discussions about your values, priorities, and aspirations for the world. Whether it's serving at the local food bank, walking dogs at a shelter, or participating in community clean-up efforts, working together towards a common goal cultivates teamwork and camaraderie. This not only builds emotional intimacy but also creates a shared understanding of each other's passions, which can be profoundly fulfilling.

Another activity that can deepen emotional intimacy is engaging in book clubs or reading together. Choose books that challenge your perspectives or evoke deep emotions. After reading, set aside time to discuss the themes, characters, and emotions that influenced you. This encourages thoughtful conversation and the sharing of personal insights. Reading literature or exploring different genres can help you both discover more about each other's thinking patterns and emotional landscapes. Each conversation can unfold layers of understanding, making your bond stronger and more resilient.

Music is another universal language that speaks volumes, and participating in musical activities together can spark intimate moments. Learn to play an instrument side by side, start a mini jam session, or embark on creating a shared playlist that reflects your relationship journey. Reflecting on the meanings behind the songs offers insight into each other's values and emotions, transforming the act of listening or performing into a deeper connection.

Fitness activities also foster intimacy through shared dedication and motivation. Whether you prefer yoga, dancing, or weekend runs, moving your bodies together enhances emotional well-being. Create shared goals in fitness, celebrating achievements together as you cheer each other on. The shared endorphin boost coupled with the opportunity to support one another during difficult workouts fosters a sense of trust and companionship.

Traveling, even if it's locally or just a weekend getaway, can release stress and invigorate relationships. New experiences bring couples closer as they navigate unfamiliar environments, enriching their emotional connection. As you explore new places, share laughter and create memories that only the two of you can hold dear. The interactions with locals or fellow travelers provide opportunities for growth and reflection on each other's perspectives, cultivating appreciation for the differences and similarities that exist in the world and within your relationship.

Lastly, creating rituals or traditions can also nurture emotional intimacy. Establishing a regular practice, whether it's a morning coffee together or an evening walk under the stars, embeds a sense of security and predictability in your relationship. These small yet meaningful rituals become cherished moments that reinforce your connection. Sharing your days, dreams, and sometimes even fears during those moments can lead to vulnerability, which fosters an even deeper emotional intimacy.

In conclusion, the pursuit of emotional intimacy in a relationship does not merely rely on physical closeness or romantic gestures. By exploring various non-sexual activities that foster connection, couples can cultivate a deeper understanding of each other, nurture shared experiences, and build lasting emotional bonds. Each activity presents a unique opportunity for partners to discover new facets of their relationship while simultaneously reinforcing their commitment to one another. Exploring hobbies, volunteering, engaging in creative pursuits, and establishing traditions—all contribute to a reservoir of shared experiences that can sustain and invigorate your intimacy long after the lights go down. Encouraging patience, openness, and communication within shared activities lays the groundwork for a relationship imbued not just with love, but with profound emotional depth that transcends the boundaries of the bedroom.

Creating a Safe Space

Creating a safe space within a relationship is one of the most fundamental aspects of fostering intimacy. This concept extends beyond the boundaries of the physical realm and seeps into the emotional and psychological landscapes that define our connections. To create an environment where both partners feel secure enough to express their vulnerabilities and desires, it is important to cultivate a foundation built on trust, understanding, and non-judgment. This subchapter will explore various dimensions of creating such a safe space, offering insights and practical strategies for couples looking to deepen their connection.

At its core, a safe space in a relationship involves the ability to communicate without fear of backlash or misunderstanding. When partners feel secure, they can express their thoughts, feelings, needs, and desires without the cloak of hesitation. This kind of openness is essential for intimacy, forming the bedrock upon which emotional connection can flourish. It can be challenging, especially in a world where vulnerability is often met with judgment or dismissal, but the rewards of establishing a safe haven for each other are immeasurable.

The journey toward creating this environment begins with mindful communication. It is imperative for both partners to approach conversations with an open heart and a willingness to listen. Instead of preparing rebuttals or getting defensive, they can focus on understanding each other's perspectives. Active listening involves not only hearing words but also recognizing underlying emotions and intentions. When partners listen genuinely, it connects them on a deeper level, ensuring that both feel valued and understood.

Establishing ground rules for discussions can be an effective way to maintain the integrity of conversations. Couples can agree on key principles, such as avoiding personal attacks, dismissive gestures, or interruptions. These ground rules create a shared understanding of how to navigate conversations safely. A common guideline is to use "I" statements when expressing feelings. For example, saying "I feel hurt when you don't acknowledge my efforts" rather than "You never appreciate anything I do" can smooth the communication process and reduce the likelihood of defensiveness.

In addition to communication, fostering emotional availability is also vital for creating a safe space. Partners must be willing to be vulnerable, sharing not only their joys and successes but also their fears, insecurities, and regrets. This shows that the relationship is a sanctuary for both partners. However, being vulnerable requires courage. The willingness to unveil one's innermost self is a gift that should be reciprocated. By demonstrating vulnerability, partners signal that it is okay to explore the less-than-perfect aspects of themselves without fear of rejection.

Creating rituals or dedicated times for check-ins can also help maintain the emotional availability necessary for a safe space. Couples might set aside time each week to discuss how they are feeling individually and collectively. This practice not only promotes intimacy but also reinforces the idea that both partners prioritize each other's emotional health. During these meetings, each person can share not only their current feelings but also express gratitude for specific actions their partner took during the week that reinforced their sense of safety and connection.

In embracing vulnerability, it's essential to recognize the power dynamics that often exist in relationships. One partner might feel more comfortable expressing their vulnerabilities due to personality traits, past experiences, or attachment styles. It's crucial to encourage the less vocal partner to share while being mindful of their comfort levels. Creating a safe space means not only the freedom to express but also ensuring that both partners have equitable opportunities to be heard. This consideration nurtures mutual respect and understanding, contributing significantly to the intimacy both partners seek.

However, while establishing an environment of openness and vulnerability is vital, it can sometimes lead to the spilling of insecurities that may overwhelm the receiving partner. This is where boundaries become paramount. Inviting one partner into a dialogue about their vulnerabilities does not mean that both partners must engage in or absorb every detail at once, especially if it may lead to emotional overload. Setting boundaries helps safeguard both partners' emotional well-being while still promoting openness.

Discussing what is comfortable to share and what remains private provides clarity and comfort. Partners can agree that certain conversations may need to be tackled gradually, especially if they delve into deeper or more painful subjects. This approach reinforces the idea that the relationship is a safe haven, allowing for shared exploration without forcing either partner into uncomfortable territory.

Encouraging each partner to express their needs in being supported also fosters a healthy balance. Some may prefer a listening ear without feedback, while others may desire advice or solutions to their problems. Clarifying these preferences can lead to more tailored support and minimize feelings of abandonment or misunderstanding. It becomes part of the art of creating a safe space—the continual adjustment to meet those needs.

In constructing a safe space, the physical environment also plays a significant role. Couples can create a sanctuary at home— where they can unwind, share openly, and communicate safely— by investing in a comforting ambiance that promotes intimacy. Consideration of lighting, furnishings, and even scents creates an atmosphere conducive to openness and connection. A cozy nook with soft pillows, calming scents, and dim lighting sets the stage for deeper conversations.

Additionally, the timing of discussions matters significantly. Approaching sensitive topics when tensions are high or during particularly stressful moments may lead to misunderstandings. On the contrary, discussing such matters during more relaxed moments, perhaps over a coffee date, can lead to more fruitful insights.

Non-verbal communication is another crucial aspect of creating a safe space. Body language, facial expressions, and even tone of voice can convey immense amounts of information. Partners can practice becoming more attuned to these signals from each other, recognizing that non-verbal cues often speak louder than words. This awareness fosters a deeper emotional connection, making both partners feel more secure and understood.

Emotional support and reassurance are indispensable to the safety of this space. Explicitly acknowledging the importance of a partner's feelings can reinforce their sense of worth and validity. Simple affirmations, words of appreciation, and acknowledgment of struggles can significantly enhance the environment of safety. A comforting phrase such as, "I hear you, and I appreciate you for sharing your feelings with me," can demonstrate that both partners actively value the vulnerability of their shared experience.

Conflict resolution is also inherent to creating a safe space. Disagreements are natural in any relationship, but how couples address them can either build or erode trust and safety. Approaching conflict with the intention to understand and connect rather than to win or defeat can keep the foundation of the safe space intact. Watching for escalating tensions and recognizing them signals a need to pause and regroup, communicating effectively is crucial.

During conflicts, it can also be helpful to engage in techniques such as taking breaks when discussions become too heated. Both partners can agree to pause the conversation, take some time to process individual feelings, and reconvene when cooler heads prevail. This break can prevent escalation and create a more conducive environment for resolution.

Embracing a spirit of curiosity also encourages openness within a safe space. Partners should cultivate a mindset open to learning from each other's perspectives. Promoting the idea that differences in feelings and opinions are opportunities to grow together rather than threats enhances intimacy. Both partners can ask questions such as, "What influenced your perspective on this?" to promote understanding and connection.

Establishing expressions of affection outside the bedroom can also solidify feelings of safety and intimacy. Simple gestures, shared laughter, or even playful teasing can foster connection and joy. Engaging in non-sexual physical affection, like cuddling or holding hands, promotes emotional warmth and reinforces bonds. These practices create a culture of safety that helps partners explore deeper intimacy when the time is right.

Creating a sense of predictability through recurring rituals or shared practices reinforces the safety of emotional exposure. Whether it's regular date nights, shared hobbies, or even morning coffee together, establishing patterns fosters stability. This stability aids in developing trust and comfort, making vulnerability feel less daunting.

Ultimately, a safe space within a relationship is about mutual respect, understanding, and love. Creating such an environment doesn't happen overnight; it is a continual dance of adjustment, responsiveness, and patience. Couples who commit to building and maintaining this aspect of their relationship will find that the rewards are profound. By cultivating an atmosphere of trust, where both partners feel secure to share their vulnerabilities and desires, they lay the groundwork for deeper connection and enduring intimacy.

In conclusion, fostering a safe space within a relationship is essential for nurturing intimacy. It involves open communication, emotional availability, establishing boundaries, and addressing the physical environment, all of which contribute to a nurturing and supportive context. By engaging in practices that promote trust and understanding, partners can create the sanctuary necessary for vulnerability to thrive, allowing their relationship to blossom into a profound connection. Each step taken towards creating this safe space signifies a commitment to emotional depth, creating a partnership that withstands the complexities of life while cherishing shared intimacy.

------ Chapter 7 ------

HEALING THROUGH INTIMACY

HEALING THROUGH INTIMACY

Using Physical Intimacy as Healing

In the landscape of relationships, physical intimacy stands out as a potent force not only for pleasure but also for healing. Emotional wounds, whether borne from past trauma or the everyday struggles of life, often manifest in ways that can erode the fabric of a relationship. Physical intimacy can provide the comfort, connection, and sense of safety needed to begin the healing process, allowing couples to navigate their complexities together.

Understanding Physical Intimacy in Healing

To understand how physical intimacy can facilitate healing, it is essential to recognize its multifaceted nature. Physical intimacy encompasses not just sexual activity but also affectionate touch, cuddling, and simple gestures like holding hands or embracing. These acts of affection open the door to vulnerability and emotional expression, allowing partners to share their feelings and fears without spoken words.

One of the core elements of physical intimacy is oxytocin, often referred to as the 'love hormone.' Released during physical touch, oxytocin fosters feelings of connection and trust, which are essential elements for healing emotional wounds. This biochemical response reinforces the bond between partners, creating a safe environment where both individuals can lower their defenses and begin to address the emotional challenges they face.

Real-Life Testimonials: Healing Through Touch

Couples' stories provide profound insights into how physical intimacy serves as a vehicle for emotional healing. Here are some testimonials that illuminate this transformative experience.

Emily and James:

Emily and James, married for five years, faced a crucial turning point after Emily experienced a significant loss in her family. The grief she bore was heavy, causing an emotional rift between them. Instead of verbalizing her pain, Emily withdrew, leading to feelings of isolation for James as well. One night, while sitting together on the couch, James gently wrapped his arms around her.

"At first, I felt like I was trapped in my own sadness, but his touch transformed that feeling. I didn't have to say anything. Just being close to him felt like my heart could breathe again," Emily shared.

That simple embrace initiated a reconnection that was vital for both of them. In the weeks that followed, building on their physical closeness, they found themselves exploring deeper conversations about emotional scars, loss, and love. The mix of comforting touch and open dialogue marked the beginning of their healing journey.

Mark and Lisa:

Mark and Lisa's relationship took a toll following Mark's deployment in the military. Upon his return, it became evident that he was carrying the weight of unresolved trauma. Lisa felt a gulf of longing for connection, coupled with frustration at Mark's emotional withdrawal.

"I had no idea how to reach him. Words seemed useless," Lisa recounted.

After much contemplation, she decided to resort to physical intimacy as a bridge to his heart. One night, during a quiet moment at home, Lisa reached for Mark's hand and held it tightly.

"We started with small touches — just holding hands, then cuddling on the couch, and it was like peeling back layers of something that was so tightly wound. Each touch seemed to unearth a little more of his pain, and we began to connect again," she explained.

Together, they navigated through Mark's experiences in a way that felt safe. Gradually, these moments evolved into deeper conversations about the challenges of his time away and what it meant for their relationship.

Types of Physical Intimacy That Heal

Physical intimacy healing includes various forms that vary based on couples' needs and preferences. Here are several types that can be particularly effective:

1. Affectionate Touch:
    Simple acts of touch, such as hugs, kisses, and holding hands, can create a powerful sense of warmth and connection. Regular affectionate touch can serve to reinforce bonds, providing a foundation upon which deeper conversations can take place.

2. Cuddling:
    Taking the time to cuddle can create a fortress of safety, allowing partners to support one another while navigating their emotional landscapes. This closeness often helps individuals feel more grounded and less alone in their struggles.

3. Sexual Intimacy:
    Engaging in sexual intimacy can act as a release of pent-up emotions. It allows for a unique blend of vulnerability and strength, wherein couples not only express love but also find solace in shared passion. Sexual intimacy often opens doors for honest discussions about personal needs and desires, fostering a deeper understanding of one another.

4. Mindful Touch:
    Practicing mindfulness during moments of intimacy can enhance the experience. Focusing on the sensations, the sounds, and the emotions present during physical closeness can deepen the connection and facilitate emotional processing.

5. Physical Affection as Support:
   For some, merely being present and offering physical support — a gentle touch on the back during a distressing moment or an arm around the shoulder — becomes crucial. Such gestures signify understanding and support, allowing partners to feel less isolated in their struggles.

The Connection Between Touch and Emotional Healing Touch activates the parasympathetic nervous system, which promotes a state of calmness and relaxation. This physiological response can be especially powerful in moments of distress, providing a refuge from anxiety. Researchers have shown that couples engaging in regular physical intimacy report feeling more satisfied and secure in their relationships, underscoring the strong correlation between emotional and physical connectivity.

By fostering a sense of safety, touch can help mitigate feelings of depression and anxiety within relationships. Many therapists advocate for incorporating more physical intimacy in sessions, emphasizing its role in reconstructing emotional health and connection.

Professional Insights on Healing Through Intimacy

Expert opinions lend additional weight to the narrative that physical intimacy can be instrumental in healing. Clinical psychologist Dr. Maya Harris emphasizes the importance of touch in her practice.

"When individuals face trauma or emotional pain, what they often need most is a compassionate connection that can be physically felt. Touch drives the emotional dialogue that can be so difficult to articulate. It allows partners to establish trust in an environment where they often feel most vulnerable," Dr. Harris explains. Moreover, sex therapist Dr. Samuel Reed reflects on the hesitation many couples feel about discussing intimacy after a traumatic experience. "It's not uncommon for partners to shy away from physical intimacy out of fear of triggering negative feelings. However, it's essential to approach touch mindfully and create an environment where healing can occur through connection," he advises.

Navigating Challenges: Healing in the Face of Resistance

While physical intimacy can be a powerful healing tool, it's not without its challenges. For some, past traumas manifest as resistance to intimacy. Navigating these waters requires empathy, patience, and understanding from both partners.

Partners may need to establish clear communication about their comfort levels, boundaries, and fears surrounding intimacy. Engaging openly during these discussions fosters trust and cultivates an atmosphere of safety. When one partner expresses discomfort, it's crucial to listen actively and respect their needs without offense or resentment.

For example, Sarah and Tom faced hurdles after Sarah disclosed her trauma from previous relationships. Sarah found being intimate extremely challenging, often associating physical touch with feelings of fear and anxiety. Rather than pushing forward, Tom actively listened, allowing Sarah to express her need for space while also assuring her of his unwavering support.

"I realized that imposing intimacy wouldn't heal her; instead, it could reinforce her fears. I had to be patient, understanding, and find ways to support her healing through gentle touch without expectations," Tom shared.

They began slowly, incorporating gestures like holding hands or sitting close, without the pressure of moving into sexual intimacy. This method of nurturing physical closeness in lower-stakes situations allowed Sarah to gradually reclaim her comfort with touch.

Building a Culture of Healing Through Intimacy

To cultivate an environment that supports healing through intimacy, couples can consciously create rituals or practices. These shared moments foster connection and reinforce emotional bonds. Here are som practical ideas that couples may consider:

1. Daily Check-ins:
   Establish a routine where partners check in with each other daily. This can be a space to share feelings, discuss challenges, or express gratitude. The emphasis on regular communication can create a sense of security, allowing couples to navigate emotions together.

2. Non-Sexual Affection:
   Encourage non-sexual forms of affection to foster intimacy without the pressure of performance. Making space for simple gestures, like hugging, cuddling, or sitting close, helps alleviate the anxiety surrounding sexual intimacy.

3. Mindfulness Practices:
   Couples can engage in mindfulness practices together, such as meditation or yoga, which promote emotional connection and awareness.

   Mindfulness-focused activities encourage attunement to each other's needs and feelings, increasing understanding and compassion.

4. Create Safe Spaces:
   Designate spaces within the home as safe zones where both partners feel comfortable expressing emotions openly. Spending time in these areas encourages emotional sharing and connection.

5. Physical Touch Routines:
   Building intimacy can be woven into daily routines through physical touch. Whether it's holding hands during a walk or a hug before bed, these habitual actions can bolster feelings of love and support.

Conclusion: The Journey Together

The journey through intimacy as a mechanism for healing is profoundly transformative. As couples engage in the multifaceted aspects of physical closeness, they create avenues for healing from within. By facilitating deeper emotional connections through love, trust, and understanding, couples can conquer the complexities of their emotional landscapes together.

Ultimately, healing is not a solitary endeavor; it thrives in partnership. The stories shared and the practices implemented reflect a commitment to nurturing each other, making space for all emotions, and embracing the tender, healing power of touch in their shared journey. In doing so, they reaffirm their love, fostering an atmosphere of intimacy that transcends physicality and fosters emotional resilience.

Emotional Support and Healing

In the ever-evolving landscape of a relationship, emotional support emerges as one of the cornerstones upon which healing is built. Intimacy is often thought of in physical terms, yet it is, in many ways, primarily an emotional endeavor. For couples navigating the complexities of trust, understanding, and vulnerability, the emotional connection between partners can either serve as a combatant against the challenges of life or as a weight that crushes the spirit. Understanding the profound impact of emotional support on healing requires us to first examine what emotional support entails. At its core, emotional support means being there for one another—not just in the moments of celebration but also in times of struggle, fear, and uncertainty. It includes acts of listening, validating feelings, and offering reassurance. This support can manifest in a myriad of ways, such as a gentle touch, a kind word, or simply the willingness to be present without judgment.

A survey of couples reveals that partners who feel emotionally supported by one another experience higher levels of relationship satisfaction. Ann and Mark, married for over a decade, took the time to reflect on how they navigated a tumultuous patch in their relationship when Ann faced health challenges.

"When I was at my lowest, Mark didn't try to fix me," Ann recalled. "He just sat with me. He held my hand, listened to my fears about the future, and shared in my tears. That emotional presence was what I needed to start healing."

Mark added, "I learned that being there didn't mean having all the answers. Sometimes, simply acknowledging her pain was enough to show that I was committed to supporting her. I wanted her to feel that she was not alone in this fight."

Listeners can often become silent observers of their partner's emotional landscape. In moments of distress, it may be tempting to jump into problem-solving mode, but this approach can often stifle healing by creating distance rather than connection. Listening deeply and empathetically allows partners to understand the complexities of one another's emotions, fostering both intimacy and resilience in the relationship as a whole.

Trust, a fundamental component of emotional support, allows partners to be vulnerable. Vulnerability is often viewed with dread, seen as a weakness; however, true strength lies in the courage to express one's hurt and insecurities. When both partners establish a trusting environment, they create a safe space where they can share openly without fear of judgment.

This symbiotic relationship between emotional support and trust enables healing in profound ways.

Taking a deeper dive into the role of trust, we find that it not only allows for raw emotional expression but also reinforces commitment. Couples who actively work on their trust levels through open communication and shared experiences tend to rebuild and strengthen their bonds.

Jenna and Brian, another couple who participated in research for this chapter, shared their experience of overcoming a significant breach of trust. "We had to rebuild what was broken, and while it was tough, we leaned into emotional support to help us through," Jenna explained. "We spent countless nights just talking, understanding one another's perspectives, and slowly writing a new story."

Brian added, "I realized that I had done hurtful things in the past that impacted Jenna's ability to trust me. I had to earn her trust back, and it wasn't a quick process. It required emotional labor and deep conversations where we faced uncomfortable truths about our relationship."

In healing, understanding becomes a vital ingredient alongside emotional support. It is through understanding that partners can interpret the emotional cues of each other and respond with compassion. When one partner is hurting, their emotional state can manifest in various ways—change in behavior, mood swings, or withdrawal from intimacy. This is where understanding transcends mere sympathy; it requires a willingness to step into the other's shoes.

Shared experiences can help deepen understanding in ways that go beyond surface-level dialogue. Couples can engage in activities that mirror the challenges faced—trust-building exercises, communication workshops, or simply sharing their own childhood stories that may reveal how past traumas shape current emotional responses. Such endeavors are not just about knowledge but are foundational steps in empathizing with one another's struggles.

Moreover, support and understanding in healing can significantly uplift partners' self-esteem. Emotional struggles can often lead to feelings of inadequacy. The care shown by a partner can be transformative, instilling a sense of worthiness.

Research illustrates that the emotional backing offered by one partner helps foster resilience in the other. When both partners are invested in bolstering one another's emotional health, they set the stage for healing that resonates well beyond individual issues.

The journey of healing can also be undertaken through everyday interactions. Simple gestures—sending a text message to check in, preparing a favorite meal, or taking a walk together—hold the potential to convey care and concern. These small actions reinforce the bond and signal an ongoing commitment to supporting one another's well-being.

Despite the beauty of emotional support, not all couples naturally exhibit these behaviors. It often requires intention and practice to develop this framework of support. Couples can start by practicing active listening during conversations, focusing on understanding rather than responding. They should create an atmosphere of safety where vulnerability is not only accepted but celebrated—where sharing fears and insecurities is met with love rather than dismissal. The input of relational therapists can also be fundamental to enhancing emotional support dynamics within a relationship. Couples counseling is an avenue where partners can better learn skills to support one another; therapists often teach clients how to practice empathy, enhance communication, and create healthy emotional boundaries. With professional guidance, partners can learn to effectively articulate their own needs while remaining attuned to their partner's emotional states, thus enriching their relational experience.

Engaging in therapeutic workshops or retreats can provide couples with deeper insights into emotional support strategies, enriched by professional coaching and the experience of other couples facing similar struggles.

As one partner begins to experience relief from emotional pain, it creates a ripple effect throughout the relationship. The emotional healing experienced by one individual often lends strength to the other, leading to collective resilience. When held in a supportive embrace, partners can face external challenges and work through internal conflicts more effectively.

Ultimately, emotional support is a journey rather than a destination. Couples must be prepared to embrace both the triumphs and setbacks they experience along the way. By committing to a shared process of healing, partners develop a collaborative mindset that transforms their relationship into a profound source of strength that reflects mutual care, respect, and understanding.

As partners navigate their journey toward healing, it's crucial that they understand that emotional support is akin to tending a garden; it requires attention, nurturing, and time to flourish. By providing consistent, compassionate care to one another, couples can cultivate an environment where healing, growth, and intimacy can thrive—allowing not just the scars to heal but for vibrant, new connections to blossom from the very places of pain.

Rediscovering Touch

In the tapestry of human connection, touch is a fundamental thread that weaves partners together, providing a language that's often more expressive than words. When couples face periods of disconnection, rediscovering that thread can become a healing journey. Touch is often considered a primary vehicle of intimacy, nurturing emotional bonds and fostering healing through physical closeness. In this subchapter, we will explore how couples can reconnect physically after experiencing emotional distances, conflicts, or trauma, offering exercises designed to help partners rekindle their physical affection in ways that are deeply healing, meaningful, and transformative.

The power of touch is rooted in our biology and psychology. Research has consistently shown that physical touch stimulates the release of oxytocin, often called the 'love hormone.' This neuropeptide, which plays a key role in social bonding, reduces levels of cortisol (the stress hormone) and increases feelings of trust and connection. For couples, especially those who may have faced adversity or emotional disconnection, prioritizing touch can be both a gentle and profound way to reconnect. Yet, the process of rediscovering touch isn't always straightforward; it often requires vulnerability, patience, and a willingness to understand each other's needs.

To embark on this journey, it helps to revisit the foundation of why touch is vital. Every couple experiences challenges, be it through life stressors, trauma, or the routine strains of everyday life, which can create emotional and physical distance. In these moments, it isn't uncommon for physical touch to diminish alongside emotional intimacy. Couples may find themselves feeling like roommates rather than lovers. Rekindling this intimacy requires intention and practice. Therefore, let's explore various exercises that can help couples rediscover touch together, reconnecting in ways that facilitate healing and intimacy.

The first exercise encourages couples to deepen their understanding of one another's preferences and boundaries regarding touch. This can be achieved through a simple yet powerful practice known as 'The Touch Agreement.' Both partners write down their preferred types and contexts for touch, as well as any areas where they might feel uncomfortable. After sharing their lists, they engage in an open conversation, discussing what touch means to them emotionally and physically. By setting the stage for a safe exchange about touch, partners are more equipped to navigate their experiences together.

Next, let's explore 'The Gentle Awakening' exercise. In this practice, couples dedicate a specific time to explore touch in a non-sexual way. Setting the scene is crucial; find a quiet space, dim the lights, and perhaps play soft music. One partner begins by gently tracing their fingers along the other's arm, shoulder, or back, moving with a deliberate slowness that focuses on sensation rather than destination. The receiving partner can close their eyes, focusing solely on the experience, which allows them to reconnect with their body and senses. After several minutes, partners switch roles. This exercise heightens awareness of physical sensations, fostering a deeper connection that precedes any sexual interaction.

Being mindful of how touch feels can make a significant difference in self-awareness and intimacy. 'Mindful Touch' is another valuable exercise, encouraging couples to engage in a practice of shared mindfulness. Partners sit facing each other, maintain eye contact, and take a few deep breaths together to create a shared atmosphere of presence. They then take turns giving each other a brief shoulder massage, focusing not just on the physical act but also on being present with their partner's experience. Observing how the other moves, feels, and responds to touch can deepen understanding and strengthen bonds.

For couples who may struggle with the concept or act of physical intimacy due to past trauma or emotional scars, creating a 'Safe Space Ritual' can be incredibly impactful. This exercise emphasizes the importance of establishing a safe and welcoming environment to engage in touch. Partners can choose a physical space in their home that embodies comfort—this could be a cozy corner of their living room or a designated area in the bedroom. In this space, they can communicate openly about their feelings regarding touch, touching visibly and intentionally, taking turns to initiate touch without the pressure of intimacy. Over time, this ritual can foster safety and trust, allowing partners to explore their comfort zones and re- engage with touch gradually.

Furthermore, the practice of 'Touch Without Expectation' allows couples to cultivate deeper physical affection absent of any sexual associations. Partners can dedicate a moment each day to simply hold hands, cuddle, or embrace, without the expectation of intimacy leading to sexual interaction. These actions promote a sense of safety and love that can permeate throughout their connection, reinforcing emotional and physical intimacy on mutually agreed terms.

For couples facing challenging conversations or conflicts, 'Healing Touch' can be extremely beneficial. This practice combines supportive touch with active listening. One partner begins by voicing their feelings about a particular issue. The listening partner can respond with light, comforting touch—perhaps an arm around the shoulder or a gentle hand on the back—while they talk. This touch serves as a reminder of their partnership and commitment to working through challenges together, rather than feeling alone in conflict.

Following satisfactory communication, couples can practice 'The Connection Dialogue' to discuss their needs regarding physical touch. Within this dialogue, each partner expresses what types of touch they find comforting and reassuring while sharing any insecurities or fears they may have. Phrasing statements such as, "I feel more connected when you hold my hand," can facilitate deeper awareness of each person's emotional and physical i n t i m a c y needs.

Exploring new forms of touch can help couples step outside their comfort zones and connect in novel ways. Activities like 'Dance Together' or 'Playful Touch' might help couples rediscover joy in physical connection. In Dance Together, partners can indulge in spontaneous dancing, whether it's following a choreographed routine or simply moving together in rhythm. The act of dancing together can lead to laughter, shared joy, and mutual understanding, reinforcing their bond.

Further expanding their experiences, 'Playful Touch' encourages couples to incorporate lightheartedness into their time together, fostering moments of playfulness. Activities could consist of pillow fights, tickling, or three-minute hug sessions, all designed to welcome laughter and joy into their interactions. Play reliefs accumulated stress in the relationship and paves the way for deeper, healing touch.

Couples may also explore the restorative practice of 'Bath or Shower Together,' which provides an intimate environment to connect physically and emotionally through warmth and touch. Sharing moments in the serene atmosphere of water serves as a gentle reminder of how touch can cleanse emotional burdens and enhance affection. Partners can work together to share massages, laughter, or simply enjoy the closeness that comes from being in a shared space.

The journey of rediscovering touch is not solely about the physical aspect but also invites couples to engage their emotional sensitivity.

Following exercises that revive physical affection, incorporating rituals of gratitude can significantly enhance the intimacy building journey. Taking time to express appreciation toward one another serves as a nurturing balm for both partners, reinforcing that their emotional and physical connection is cherished and valued. Incorporating simple practices—like voicing what they love about each other or recording mutual strengths—can significantly shift the dynamics of touch from merely transactional to deeply meaningful.

For couples who recognize the emotional blocks to touch, it may be necessary to address these challenges in more structured ways. Utilizing 'Guided Touch' can serve as an effective approach, in which couples work with a therapist specializing in relationships and intimacy. Guided sessions promote a safe environment to discuss discomforts surrounding touch, allowing partners to address their vulnerabilities in tandem. This structured support provides strategies to help couples navigate through difficult emotions, readjust expectations, and foster healing and supportive physical closeness.

As couples progress in their rediscovery of touch, discussion around intimacy can shift toward future goals and aspirations. 'Future Visioning' encourages partners to visit their long-term aspirations as a couple concerning their intimacy and physical connection. Using visual aids—such as vision boards—can become a fun and inspiring engagement activity where they visualize their goals for physical connection in new experiences, role of touch in their lives, and develop shared objectives about learning and enhancing their emotional and ergonomic intimacy.

Ultimately, the act of rediscovering touch is steeped in intention and commitment. Couples must approach this healing journey with openness, patience, and understanding. Historical barriers to intimacy may not vanish overnight, and it's essential to remember that small steps can lead to significant changes. Partners should celebrate the milestones they achieve together, whether it be overcoming a hesitation to initiate touch or reaching a moment of vulnerability that leads to deeper closeness. Through this conscious endeavor, partners have the potential to move beyond mere physical affection and create a healing space where true emotional intimacy blossoms.

As partners engage in this journey of rediscovery, it's crucial to remain attuned to one another's evolving needs and experiences. Each exercise fosters openness for growth, adaptation, and trust while the couple establishes a new rhythm in their relationship. This journey reminds couples that touch is not merely an act but a genuine expression of love, connection, and healing. Through the act of physically reconnecting, couples can nurture not only their relationship but also each other's heart and soul, leading them toward a beautifully intertwined, intimate tapestry.

—— Chapter 8 ——

THE ROLE OF TRUST

Foundation of Trust

Trust is often described as the foundation upon which strong relationships are built. Just as a house necessitates a solid structure to endure storms, relationships thrive when they are fortified by mutual trust. This subchapter delves deeply into the importance of trust as the bedrock of intimacy, exploring how it is cultivated and sustained within partnerships. Throughout this exploration, we will hear stories from couples who have navigated the often-turbulent waters of trust, sharing their insights on how they fostered a dependable emotional landscape conducive to closeness.

At its core, trust in a relationship embodies a reliance on one another's integrity, ability, and character. It signifies the belief that one's partner has their interests at heart and will remain loyal, supportive, and faithful. This commitment fosters safety, inviting partners to express their deepest selves without fear of judgment or betrayal. Through trust, intimacy burgeons; emotional closeness feels natural, and vulnerability can be embraced rather than feared.

Consider the journey of Sarah and Mark. Married for over a decade, they began their relationship cloaked in the initial excitement and passion of new love. Yet as time passed, they faced a series of challenges that threatened their trust. A growing sense of disconnect began to creep into their daily exchanges as careers consumed their energies, leaving little room for open communication. It wasn't until a pivotal moment—Mark's unexpected job loss—that the couple recognized the cracks in their foundation.

In the wake of that loss, the couple had a stark choice to make: to withdraw further into their individual worlds or to trust each other with their vulnerabilities. Choosing vulnerability, Sarah encouraged Mark to share his fears about the future, while Mark, in turn, made space for Sarah to express her frustration at the tension their situation had created.

"I think the hardest part was admitting that we were both scared," Sarah shared during a recent conversation. "Trust wasn't just about being faithful; it was about trusting that we could face these obstacles together." Their commitment to honest communication enabled them to strengthen their trust, underpinning their intimacy. They developed a nightly practice of sharing their thoughts and feelings about their days and aspirations, fostering a renewed sense of partnership.

As their relationship evolved, they discovered that trust is not a static entity but rather a dynamic process that requires constant nurturing. Their journey underscores the necessity of proactive engagement in building trust. Affirmations of loyalty came not just through promises but through daily actions—supporting one another in life's endeavors, celebrating achievements, and offering comfort in times of distress.

While every couple's experience with trust is unique, there are universal principles that can guide partners in establishing a reliable emotional framework. First and foremost, honesty is essential. Couples who cultivate trust must prioritize truthfulness, even when it is uncomfortable. In their interactions, Sarah and Mark learned that sugarcoating reality or avoiding tough conversations eroded their trust over time. Open discussions about feelings, fears, and insecurities laid the groundwork for deeper connections, allowing them to feel seen and heard.

Another critical element to nurturing trust is consistency. Trust flourishes when partners exhibit reliable behavior over time. "It's about showing up, even in the little things," Mark explained. "If I say I'll do something, I need to follow through." Consistency establishes dependability, reinforcing the idea that partners can rely on one another. In this way, small gestures of support culminate in a robust bond, producing a sense of safety that protects against insecurities.

To illustrate this point further, let's explore the story of Ana and Juan, who faced significant hurdles in their early years of marriage. Ana struggled with anxiety, which sometimes manifested as envy related to Juan's social interactions outside of their home. This emotional unrest created tension that threatened their bond, as Ana's fears would occasionally lead her to confront Juan, questioning his commitments and intentions.

Recognizing the detrimental impact of these confrontations, Juan sought to reinforce his reliability. "I had to show Ana that she was my priority," he reflected. "That meant being transparent about my social plans and including her in them wherever possible." By sharing his feelings candidly and actively inviting Ana into his world, Juan began to alleviate her fears, demonstrating consistency in his commitment to their relationship. Their trust began to blossom, allowing them to cultivate greater intimacy and emotional safety.

Restoration of trust can also be crucial when missteps occur. Every relationship will inevitably encounter moments of betrayal or disappointment. Jennifer and Tom experienced this firsthand when Tom made a poor choice that jeopardized Jennifer's trust. In that instance, the couple faced the arduous task of rebuilding what had been damaged.

To recover, Tom took full accountability for his actions, illustrating the importance of transparency in the rebuilding process. He made a commitment to be open about his feelings and intentions moving forward, while Jennifer expressed her pain and disappointment candidly. Healing required time and patience, but through consistent efforts—friendlier gestures and sincere communication—Jennifer gradually learned to trust Tom again. "It was about being vulnerable enough to show my hurt and also trusting him to show me he was sorry," she noted.

This experience highlighted that trust can be reestablished, provided both partners are willing to engage in the often-challenging work of emotional reconciliation. The process reinforced the idea that compromise, accountability, and ongoing communication are paramount in nurturing a relationship defined by trust.

In some cases, however, couples may find themselves struggling with underlying issues of trust that are not directly tied to their current relationship. This was particularly true for James and Morgan, whose challenges stemmed from past relationships that had left scars. Both had experienced betrayal, and these unresolved feelings sometimes crept into their current partnership.

James found himself hesitant to communicate his fears, concerned that sharing his insecurities might lead to conflict. Morgan, on the other hand, frequently wrestled with feelings of inadequacy, which manifested in jealousy towards James's friendships. They soon realized that to move past these feelings, they needed to confront their individual histories head-on.

They began individual counseling to address their past traumas while committing to share key insights with one another. "Learning about my own triggers helped me understand Morgan better," James shared. As they navigated those difficult conversations together, they discovered mutual vulnerabilities that enabled them to forge a deeper connection.

Building trust often entails recognizing and respecting boundaries. Susan and Eric provide a poignant example of how a healthy boundary system can create fertile ground for intimacy. In their relationship, both partners actively acknowledged their individual needs and preferences regarding emotional disclosures. Susan appreciated time alone to process her feelings, while Eric valued discussing challenges openly and immediately.

"Initially, we found ourselves in conflict because I was pushing Susan to share when she wasn't ready," Eric explained. "But as we started to set boundaries for each other, we created a space where both of our needs could coexist." Respecting these boundaries enhanced their trust significantly, resulting in a more profound emotional connection. They learned that by empowering each other to honor their preferences, they could engage more deeply and vulnerably over time.

The journey of trust within relationships can also be enhanced by shared experiences that strengthen the bond between partners. Leah and Chris offer valuable insight into how companionship fosters trust. They made it a priority to engage in activities they both enjoyed, from traveling to cooking classes.

"Building memories together created an unshakeable bond," Leah stated. "The more adventures we had, the more we realized we could rely on each other in every situation." Through shared experiences, an unspoken understanding emerged, amplifying their sense of partnership. Their interactions during fun moments allowed them to forge a collaborative connection, reinforcing trust through enjoyment and camaraderie.

In times of distress, having shared memories to draw upon can remind couples of their capacity to overcome challenges together. For couples like Leah and Chris, the ability to navigate tough conversations or overcome external pressures becomes less daunting when positioned within the context of a trusting relationship.

As we explore the myriad facets of trust, it becomes essential to acknowledge that the journey is not linear. There will be highs and lows in every relationship, and trust may waver during life's unpredictable events. However, a commitment to understanding the importance of trust can provide couples with the resilience needed to weather storms.

In conclusion, the foundation of trust forms the bedrock of intimacy in relationships. Through the stories of various couples, we have seen how trust is built, maintained, and, at times, rebuilt with effort, honesty, consistency, and vulnerability. Recognizing the role that mutual accountability plays, couples can embrace challenges as opportunities for growth, fostering deeper emotional connections.

Trust invites partners to experience vulnerability as a strength rather than a weakness, opening avenues for enduring closeness. By continually nurturing this foundation, couples can cultivate a thriving relationship characterized by intimacy, joy, and resilience. The journey of trust may be complex, yet the rewards of a deeply interconnected partnership are immeasurable.

Trust-Building Strategies

Building trust within a relationship is a dynamic and ongoing process, essential for fostering intimacy and connection. In this subchapter, we will explore practical, actionable strategies that couples can employ to enhance trust, focus on transparency, and establish accountability. By implementing these strategies, partners can navigate their relationship more effectively, reinforcing the bond that underpins their emotional and physical closeness.

At the heart of trust-building lies open communication. This entails not only sharing thoughts and feelings but also creating a safe environment for both partners to express themselves honestly. Couples must prioritize discussions where both individuals feel heard and validated. This approach assists in dismantling barriers that may obstruct trust.

One fundamental strategy for enhancing transparency is setting aside regular check-in times. These can be structured weekly or biweekly meetings where couples can discuss their feelings, concerns, and any issues arising in their relationship. During these check-ins, it is critical to establish rules of openness and respect. Partners should encourage vulnerability by actively listening and responding thoughtfully.

To facilitate these discussions, consider using a 'talking stick' or a similar object to designate the individual who has the floor. This can prevent interruptions and promote attentive listening. Each partner should have an opportunity to speak without interruption, fostering a sense of security and a deeper understanding of one another's perspectives.

During these sessions, it's important to approach discussions from a place of curiosity rather than judgment. Instead of making accusations or definitive statements, ask open-ended questions. For example, "Can you help me understand how you feel about our current schedules?" This technique invites partners to share their feelings without feeling defensive.

In tackling transparency, another effective strategy is to practice radical honesty. This means committing to tell the truth in all situations, even when it might be difficult or uncomfortable. Radical honesty builds trust because it shows a willingness to be upfront about emotions, needs, and desires. It illustrates that both partners are committed to a relationship where authenticity is valued.

However, implementing radical honesty requires careful navigation. It's vital to balance honesty with kindness. Consider the phrasing of your truth—focus on expressing feelings and needs rather than making critical statements. Instead of saying, "You always forget our plans," try rephrasing it to, "I feel disappointed when our plans change unexpectedly. Can we find a way to communicate better about this?" This subtle difference reframes the conversation in a constructive way.

Alongside transparency, accountability plays a crucial role in trust-building. To establish accountability, couples must agree on individual responsibilities concerning their relationship. This can involve defining roles in mutual decision-making, personal commitments to improve specific behaviors, and being reliable in fulfilling promises.

An effective practice in enhancing accountability is to establish mutual agreements or contracts. Together, outline what each partner is committed to doing for the relationship. For instance, it could be as straightforward as agreeing to spend at least three evenings a week together without distractions. These agreements should also include how to communicate if one partner is struggling to meet their obligations. By establishing these shared goals, partners create a sense of partnership and shared responsibility.

In building this accountability framework, it is also important to create a system of consequences for unmet agreements. This doesn't mean punishing each other but rather discussing and recognizing the impact of failing to follow through. Revisit these conversations regularly to assess how well each partner is adhering to the agreements, discussing any obstacles they may face, and strategizing solutions together.

Another vital aspect of accountability is acknowledging and owning mistakes. If one partner realizes they've disappointed the other or failed to honor an agreement, it's essential to address the situation promptly. Sincerely apologize without excuses, expressing an understanding of how the action affected the other partner. This humility strengthens trust, as it demonstrates a commitment to the relationship and reinforces that each partner is invested in fostering a strong bond.

Furthermore, trust thrives on reliability. Couples should strive to be consistent with their words and actions. This means following through on promises, remembering significant dates, and being present during moments that matter. When partners can rely on each other to show up and be there when needed, it solidifies their connection.

To enhance reliability, consider creating a shared calendar or planner. This can help both partners track commitments, appointments, and important dates within their relationship. This simple tool fosters accountability by ensuring that important events and responsibilities are not overlooked, reinforcing a sense of partnership.

Additionally, consider practicing ongoing appreciation for one another. Acknowledge your partner's efforts and express gratitude for the ways they contribute to the relationship. This can be as simple as saying, "I appreciate that you took care of dinner tonight," or "Thank you for being patient while I vented about my day." Verbal affirmations nurture an atmosphere of support and connectedness, which is crucial for laying a foundation of trust.

On the flip side, becoming aware of and addressing triggers is imperative. Sometimes, certain behaviors or situations can lead to feelings of mistrust or discomfort. Open conversations about these triggers can aid in establishing a deeper understanding of one another's feelings and vulnerabilities. Creating a safety plan for what to do when those triggers occur can also lessen anxiety and foster trust.

For instance, if one partner feels anxious when the other is late coming home, discuss the situation openly. Acknowledge that such a situation may provoke insecurities related to trust. Establish a shared understanding, such as sending a quick text if there will be a delay, fosters reassurance and clarity.

In moments when trust is tested, whether due to falters in communication, unmet expectations, or external stressors, couples need to engage in repair efforts. These are deliberate actions taken to mend the relationship after trust has been shaken. A simple way to start this is through a sincere conversation aimed at rebuilding the emotional connection. This can include expressing how the situation made each partner feel while emphasizing a desire to move forward positively.

Employing vulnerability as a tool can also enhance trust-building. Sharing fears, insecurities, and personal stories can forge a deeper bond, demonstrating to each partner that they are not alone in their challenges. Vulnerability invites intimacy and understanding into the relationship, creating an environment where both parties feel safe to express themselves fully.

As couples navigate this journey towards deeper trust, it may be beneficial to engage in counseling or therapy. An objective third party can offer valuable insights and strategies, guiding couples through complex issues. This environment fosters healthy communication and accountability strategies that partners may not have considered.

In resolving conflict, remember that the goal is not to win an argument but to understand each other better. Approaching disagreements with a collaborative mindset encourages couples to explore each other's perspectives, which strengthens the foundation of trust.

Regularly revisiting the goals set regarding trust and accountability is necessary for ensuring both partners remain aligned in their efforts. It allows space for monitoring progress and identifying additional strategies that may need to be implemented. Sometimes, it becomes easy to fall back into routines, and having regular reviews motivates couples to continue nurturing their relationship.

Finally, celebrate your successes along the way. Every small victory in building trust—a successful conversation, a moment of vulnerability, or an instance of accountability—deserves acknowledgment. These celebrations reinforce the positive work both partners are doing and help build momentum for continued growth.

In conclusion, enhancing trust within a relationship requires dedication to transparency and accountability, alongside ongoing communication and respect. By employing these strategies, partners can work together to strengthen their connection and create a more intimate partnership. Continually nurturing trust enhances the foundation of a relationship, allowing both individuals to feel secure and valued. Ultimately, the effort invested in building trust is profoundly rewarding, as it deepens intimacy and fosters a robust, resilient partnership.

Rebuilding Trust After Breach

Rebuilding trust after a breach is one of the most challenging aspects of any relationship. Whether the breach was due to infidelity, dishonesty, or even a significant disagreement, the resulting emotional fracture can feel insurmountable. Yet, many couples find that with dedication and the right approach, it is possible to mend the wounds, learn from the experience, and emerge stronger together. In this subchapter, we will explore practical strategies and insights that can guide couples through this delicate journey

A trust breach can leave partners feeling shattered and vulnerable. Emotions such as betrayal, sadness, and anger often surface, creating a complex landscape of feelings to navigate. Each partner may react differently, compounding the difficulty of the situation. During this critical time, it is essential to establish effective communication and create an environment conducive to healing.

Understanding the Impact of Breach

To begin the process of healing, it is vital to comprehend the depth of the impact that a trust breach inflicts on both partners. Often, when trust is broken, it not only shatters the existing bond between the couple, it can also spark a myriad of insecurities and fears that were previously buried. Unpacking these feelings can be overwhelming but is crucial in the rebuilding process.

For the partner who feels betrayed, the experience can trigger a rollercoaster of emotions. They might grapple with feeling unworthy, questioning their judgment, and dealing with an influx of negative thoughts. It is normal for individuals to wonder about the reasons behind the betrayal and analyze the relationship's dynamics. Both partners need to acknowledge these feelings and articulate them honestly.

On the other hand, the partner who committed the breach often experiences guilt, shame, and fear of losing the relationship. They must confront their behavior's consequences while navigating their partner's emotional state. It is essential for both partners to address these feelings openly, fostering compassion and understanding as they take their first steps toward rebuilding trust.

Creating a Safe Space for Dialogue

Before diving into deep discussions about the breach, both partners must foster a safe emotional environment. This means setting ground rules for communication that prioritize honesty, respect, and emotional safety. Couples can mediate these conversations by agreeing to speak calmly, avoiding blame, and allowing each other to share feelings without interruption.

Establishing a safe space is instrumental in ensuring both partners can freely express their emotions. It's important to remember that discussions about trust breaches can become heated, as they tap into raw emotions and unresolved issues. Partners should commit to patience and understanding, even during difficult moments. Taking turns to speak and listen may also help each person feel valued, promoting a more productive dialogue.

Intentionally scheduling time to talk about the breach can also create an emotional container where both partners know they can express themselves. Setting aside distractions, choosing a quiet location, and agreeing not to resolve every issue in one sitting can provide the necessary space for genuine conversation.

Taking Responsibility and Acknowledging the Breach

Acknowledgment is often the first step towards rebuilding trust. The partner involved in the breach must take full responsibility for their actions. This means being honest without offering excuses or justifications, which can further damage the trust dynamic. Expressing sincere remorse is crucial, and it should come across as authentic, demonstrating a genuine understanding of the pain caused.

For example, if infidelity occurred, the partner who engaged in the behavior must not only acknowledge the act itself but also the emotional devastation it inflicted on their spouse. This includes recognizing how it affected the couple's dynamic and the trust they had built. To rebuild trust, the remorseful partner should be willing to share their decision-making process and foundational reasons behind their actions, allowing their partner insight into their thoughts and feelings.

Emotional Transparency and Vulnerability

A pivotal aspect of rebuilding trust is cultivating emotional transparency. Both partners must commit to being forthright about their feelings and experiences. This means sharing not just the surface-level emotions but also the fears and insecurities that may arise during this challenging time.

For the partner who breached trust, vulnerability is key. They must provide reassurance of their commitment to the relationship while expressing their hopes for the future. By sharing their emotions openly, they allow their partner to see their struggles and efforts towards betterment, which can be comforting.

Conversely, the partner who felt betrayed also has a responsibility to articulate their needs, feelings, and expectations moving forward. This shared vulnerability can eliminate walls between partners, slowly but surely rebuilding a sense of trust and partnership. Emotional transparency invites connection and helps restore the foundation that may have been disrupted.

Setting Boundaries and Expectations

An essential part of the rebuilding process is establishing clear boundaries and expectations moving forward. Discussing what both partners need in order to heal and regain trust is foundational. For the partner who was betrayed, this can include clarifying what behaviors feel safe and what does not. The partner who breached trust should be open to these requests and ready to engage in honest discussions regarding boundaries.

Setting boundaries allows both partners to express their newfound comfort levels and fosters accountability. For example, they may agree to regular check-ins about feelings and progress during their journey. This can also help reinforce commitment to one another while addressing any lingering feelings about the breach.

Mutual goal-setting can further strengthen this phase of healing. Discussing how partners envision the future of their relationship gives each person a voice in its direction. It encourages a sense of teamwork and allows couples to work collaboratively towards a healthier, more trusting relationship.

Restoring Trust on a Day-to-Day Basis

Rebuilding trust is not a linear process; it takes considerable time and effort. Adopting daily practices can support the restoration of trust and foster deeper connection. Small gestures can become profound expressions of commitment, helping partners feel secure and loved as they rebuild.

Consistency is key in restoring trust. The partner who breached trust must demonstrate reliability and follow through oncommitments. This may include doing what they say they will do, reinforcing a sense of dependability in the relationship. It may involve being present and attentive in daily interactions, signaling that both partners are committed to the process.

Additionally, engaging in shared activities can act as a fertile ground for reconnecting emotionally. Quality time spent together helps reinforce the partnership, offering opportunities to create positive experiences and memories. Trying new hobbies or simply enjoying date nights can help couples divert their focus from the breach and allow them to engage with each other anew.

Practicing Forgiveness

Forgiveness is a critical aspect of the healing process, both for the partner who felt betrayed and for the partner who breached trust. Forgiveness does not mean forgetting or dismissing the pain caused but rather releasing the hold that past grievances have on the present relationship. It's an ongoing process that requires patience and commitment from both partners.

The partner who was betrayed must actively work on letting go of resentment, which can be debilitating to the relationship. This could involve reflecting on the reasons for the breach and recognizing that the relationship can grow stronger despite past wounds. Writing down feelings, processing emotions through therapy, or discussing with friends can all be helpful tools in this journey.

The partner who breached trust should acknowledge the difficult feelings their actions have caused and be patient as their partner navigates their path to forgiveness. It's essential to foster an understanding atmosphere, encouraging open discussions about feelings without rushing the forgiveness process.

Seeking Professional Support

Couples may find it beneficial to seek professional help during the rebuilding phase. Therapists or relationship coaches can offer neutral perspectives and constructive strategies, providing a structured environment to address lingering feelings about the breach. Facilitated dialogue can also help couples communicate more effectively while learning new tools to enhance their relationship.

Therapists often work with couples to identify patterns and behaviors that contribute to their challenges, including trust issues. Through guided discussions, the couple can explore their emotional landscape, uncovering the roots of their struggles and obtaining tailored techniques for improvement.

Support groups geared towards relationship challenges can be another option. Hearing from others who have walked a similar path can foster a sense of connection and reduce feelings of isolation. Sharing experiences with others can validate a couple's journey and encourage them to persevere.

Embracing the Journey Together

Rebuilding trust is not merely about recovering from a breach; rather, it embodies a journey of growth and resilience as a couple. Throughout the process, partners should celebrate small victories, recognizing each step towards healing that contributes to their relationship.

As trust is rebuilt, couples may find themselves not only mending their relationship but also discovering deeper levels of intimacy and connection. The experience of facing adversity together can foster a profound bond, reminding partners that they are capable of overcoming challenges.

A couple's journey toward rebuilding trust may have its ups and downs, requiring flexibility and a willingness to embrace change. By committing to the process, maintaining open communication, and practicing vulnerability, partners can grow stronger together. They can savor the lessons learned, fortifying their relationship as they evolve and build a more resilient future.

In conclusion, rebuilding trust after a breach is a complex but achievable goal. It demands dedication, honesty, and vulnerability from both partners. By navigating this terrain with care, establishing clarity, and embracing support when need be, couples can emerge from their struggles with a healthier, more robust relationship. Together, they can transform the pain of a trust breach into an opportunity for profound emotional connection and intimacy.

---- Chapter 9 ----

NAVIGATING DIFFERENCES

NAVIGATING DIFFERENCES

Understanding Each Other's Needs

Understanding each other's needs in the context of intimacy is one of the most vital yet challenging tasks couples can face. Intimacy is a complex tapestry woven from various threads: emotional connection, sexual desire, vulnerability, and respect. Each person brings their own experiences, expectations, and desires to the relationship, making it crucial for couples to navigate these differences in a constructive manner.

To embark on this journey of understanding, we must first acknowledge that intimacy is not a one-size-fits-all experience. What one partner craves may differ vastly from what the other needs. For some, intimacy may mean frequent physical closeness and sexual activity, while others may find emotional bonding through shared experiences and dialogues to be equally or even more vital. Thus, fostering an environment where both partners can openly discuss their intimacy needs is paramount.

Engaging in open dialogues sets the stage for deeper understanding. Start by scheduling a time when both partners can focus solely on this conversation without distractions. This may mean setting aside a cozy evening with no screens, or perhaps taking a walk together in a quiet environment. The key is to create a safe space; an opportunity to listen and to be heard without judgment or defensiveness.

Begin the discussion by each partner sharing their perspectives on intimacy. It is essential to approach this conversation with openness and curiosity instead of assumptions or conclusions. For instance, one partner can initiate by saying, "I've been thinking about how we connect intimately, and I'd love to understand your thoughts and feelings on that subject." This invitation opens the door to a dialogue rather than a debate.

As each partner shares, they should aim for specificity instead of generalities. Using concrete examples can elucidate feelings and needs. Instead of simply stating, "I want more intimacy," one might express, "I feel closer to you when we share moments like our movie nights or weekend walks; it makes me crave more physical closeness."

While sharing, it's important to avoid phrases that could elicit defensiveness or guilt. Statements that begin with "You make me feel…" or "You always…" can lead to a reactive response. Instead, using "I" statements helps to focus on personal feelings, which can facilitate a more fruitful discussion. For instance, saying, "I feel anxious when we go several days without physical affection" can encourage understanding rather than a defensive stance.

After articulating personal needs, the conversation should shift toward understanding the partner's perspective. This requires active listening — a skill that is particularly crucial in discussions about intimacy. Active listening involves not just hearing the words but also processing the emotions behind them. This means maintaining eye contact, nodding in acknowledgment, and refraining from interrupting.

To further enhance understanding, couples can ask follow-up questions after each partner has shared their views. Questions such as, "Can you tell me more about what you need when it comes to intimacy?" or "How does that make you feel?" delve deeper into the discussion and provide clarity. This practice cultivates empathy and allows for a greater understanding of each partner's desires and boundaries.

It's vital to recognize and validate each other's feelings. Every need expressed by one partner is legitimate and deserves to be respected, even if it's different from the other's needs. Acknowledgment can come in many forms, from verbal affirmations to simple gestures of understanding, like holding hands or offering a reassuring smile. Validation does not require agreement; instead, it entails recognizing the needs as worthy of consideration.

As the conversation evolves, couples may encounter differences that could lead to tension. This is normal and should not derail the discussion. Instead, approach any friction as an opportunity for growth. When disagreements arise, it can be helpful to take a step back and remember the goal: a mutual understanding and a shared intimacy. Techniques such as taking a break for a few moments to gather thoughts or even returning to the conversation later can prevent escalation.

Beyond just discussing needs, couples should explore each other's love languages. Understanding how each partner expresses and receives love can enhance the connection significantly. According to Dr. Gary Chapman, author of "The 5 Love Languages," people generally express and feel love through five primary languages: words of affirmation, acts of service, receiving gifts, quality time, and physical touch. Having a discussion about these languages can shed light on how intimacy needs might be expressed differently and can provide new avenues for connection. For instance, if one partner's love language is physical touch, they may feel more intimate through cuddling and affection, whereas another partner whose love language is quality time may prioritize engaging discussions as a way to foster emotional intimacy.

Once both partners have a solid understanding of their intimacy needs and love languages, the next step involves setting realistic expectations and compromises. It is essential to accept that fulfilling both partners' needs may not happen overnight. Relationships require continuous communication and effort to strike a balance. This process often involves trial and error as couples discover what works best for them.

Engaging in 'intimacy check-ins' can significantly benefit couples. These are scheduled moments where partners can reflect on their intimacy levels, express any updated needs, or discuss concerns. Check-ins provide an opportunity for couples to address intimacy as a constantly evolving element of the relationship instead of a stagnant one. This approach can facilitate ongoing discussions and foster a culture of understanding, leading to a healthier and more fulfilling intimate relationship.

Ultimately, the journey of understanding each other's needs is a continuous process. It requires patience, empathy, and a willingness to navigate the unknown. Both partners need to prioritize learning about each other, creating an atmosphere where differences are celebrated rather than criticized. As couples invest in this exploration—discussing desires, setting boundaries, and embracing compromise—they lay a solid foundation for intimacy built on mutual respect and understanding.

It's important to remember that each partner's needs may evolve as the relationship matures. What's fulfilling and satisfying may change with time, influenced by life experiences, emotional growth, or changing circumstances. Therefore, returning to the fundamental practice of dialogue and sharing should be a consistent endeavor. Allowing space to revisit intimacy needs fosters a resilient bond that can adapt and flourish through all of life's changes.

Self-awareness is another critical component to navigate differences in intimacy needs. Each partner should take time to contemplate their own desires, motivations, and boundaries before entering discussions with their partner. Being introspective allows for more meaningful communication and a clearer understanding of what one seeks and needs from their partner.

In addition to self-awareness, consider the role that external influences play on intimacy needs. Stress from work, family expectations, or societal pressures can impact how individuals express themselves intimately. Recognizing these influences within the context of the discussion—by expressing thoughts like, "I've been feeling overwhelmed with work lately, and it leaves me less open to intimacy"—can provide essential context, allowing for empathy from the partner.

The path to understanding each other's needs is undoubtedly woven with challenges. However, the rewards of navigating these differences are worth the effort. Couples who commit to this understanding cultivate deeper emotional connections, creating a safe space where each partner feels valued and fulfilled. As partners evolve, so too can their intimacy—transforming into something beautiful, multifaceted, and tailored to the unique cadence of their relationship.

To further enhance understanding, partners can consider engaging in workshops or reading literature focused on intimacy and relationship dynamics. There are countless resources available from relationship experts that can provide additional insights and techniques for navigating intimacy. A professional perspective can offer new tools for couples to enhance their dialogues about needs and desires.

Thus, if you're standing at the crossroads of intimacy navigation, take the steps to understand each other's needs with open hearts and minds. Your relationship offers a unique canvas, rich with opportunities for connection, communication, and growth. Embrace this journey, for it promises to lead to a deeper and more fulfilling bond.

Through perspectives shared, vulnerability embraced, and the continuous pursuit of understanding, intimacy can transform into a harmonious dance—one that nurtures and strengthens the bond between partners even amidst their differences.

Negotiating Preferences

Navigating differences in intimacy preferences is an integral part of maintaining a healthy, fulfilling relationship. Couples often come to the table with differing desires, shaped by individual experiences, backgrounds, and even biological factors. These differences can lead to misunderstandings and feelings of disappointment if not managed in a constructive manner. As partners, engaging in respectful negotiation regarding these preferences is essential not only for enhancing intimacy but also for fostering a deep sense of connection and understanding. This subchapter aims to provide practical strategies for couples to negotiate their preferences diplomatically and openly, ultimately finding common ground and deeper intimacy.

The first step in negotiating preferences involves open dialogue. Many couples feel hesitant to initiate these discussions due to fear of rejection or conflict. However, it is essential to understand that open communication serves as the cornerstone of any successful negotiation. Each partner must feel safe and supported to express their preferences, desires, and concerns. This can be achieved by establishing a specific time to talk where both partners can focus and prepare for an honest conversation. During this time, it is crucial to create an inviting environment, free of distractions, where both individuals feel comfortable.

To initiate the discussion, one partner may begin by expressing their feelings or preferences gently. For instance, rather than stating, "You never want to try anything new," one might say,

"I've been thinking about how we connect intimately and would love to explore something new together." This gentle approach paves the way for a constructive discussion rather than placing blame.

Active listening is a vital component of open dialogue. Each partner must commit to listening without interrupting and validating the other's feelings. This encourages a sense of respect between both parties. For example, if one partner expresses a desire for more affection, the response should not be dismissive. Instead, respond with something like, "I hear that you're feeling a need for more connection through physical affection. I appreciate you sharing that with me." Acknowledging each other's feelings can help to build bridges rather than barriers.

After initiating the conversation, it's essential to explore each other's perspectives further. This may include asking open-ended questions that encourage elaboration on preferences. Queries such as, "Can you tell me more about what specific actions make you feel most connected?" can yield deeper insights into each other's needs. The goal is to understand the 'why' behind each partner's desires. Knowing the motivations can illuminate underlying issues, leading to more thoughtful negotiations.

Once both partners have shared their preferences and perspectives, it's crucial to frame the conversation around compromise. Compromise does not mean settling for less but rather finding a mutually acceptable solution that honors both parties' desires. This can involve brainstorming creative solutions together. For instance, if one partner prefers spontaneity in intimacy while the other values consistency, the couple could explore scheduling undisturbed time together while also reserving spontaneous moments. Designating certain days as 'date nights' can allow for both planned intimacy and the freedom to explore surprise encounters.

Another practical tip for negotiating preferences is to establish "intimacy check-ins." These can be regular, informal discussions where partners evaluate their relationship's intimacy landscape. For example, at the end of every week, discuss which intimate moments felt fulfilling and which could be improved. This ongoing dialogue creates a culture of transparency, where both partners can share their experiences comfortably and adjust accordingly.

Expressing gratitude is also an essential part of the negotiation process. When a partner makes an effort to accommodate another's desires, recognizing and appreciating that effort fosters positivity. Simple affirmations like, "I really enjoyed our time together last night; I felt very connected to you," serve to reinforce that the desired adjustments are not only seen but valued. Gratitude nourishes trust and creates an environment conducive to further negotiation in the future.

Moving beyond individual desires, couples should also discuss their relationship goals concerning intimacy. Aligning on broader objectives helps frame individual desires within the context of the relationship itself. For instance, partners may share a goal of enhancing emotional intimacy. This overarching goal can guide negotiations, as each partner can explore how their individual preferences contribute to achieving that goal.

When negotiating preferences, it's vital to be honest about personal limits. Sometimes, individuals may compromise only to their own detriment. If a partner is asked to engage in an intimate act that makes them uncomfortable, it's essential to articulate those feelings rather than acquiesce out of fear of conflict. Prepare responses like, "I appreciate you sharing that with me, but I feel uncomfortable with that specific request. Can we discuss an alternative that we both feel good about?"

Additionally, recognizing the difference in communication styles can aid discussions immensely. Some individuals might articulate their desires quite directly, while others may be more reserved. Understanding and adapting to these styles can significantly enhance the negotiation process. If one partner is more reticent, the other can gently encourage sharing without pressuring. Phrasing like, "I appreciate it when you share your thoughts; I want to understand you better," can help create a more conducive environment for dialogue.

When preferences stem from past experiences, they may carry emotional weight. Therefore, discussing past experiences related to intimacy can be enlightening for both partners. For example, if a partner wishes to avoid certain practices because of prior trauma, understanding this can lead to more empathetic responses. Couples should remain informed about each other's histories while negotiating, ensuring emotional sensitivity during discussions.

A productive strategy is to engage in role-playing scenarios, offering partners a safe space to explore different preferences without pressure. In these scenarios, both partners can articulate their desires and practice working towards compromise while having fun.

Role-playing can also help a couple to explore the other partner's perspective in a more direct manner, fostering better understanding.

As couples grow and evolve over time, it is important to anticipate and remain open to changes in preferences. What feels fulfilling can shift as partners age, face new life stages, or experience life's challenges. Annual or semi-annual relationship reviews can help facilitate discussions about such changes and enable couples to negotiate adjustments to their intimate life. This proactive approach can help cultivate an effective means of navigating changing preferences over time.

At times, disagreements during negotiations can lead to frustration or animosity. It's crucial to focus on resolving conflicts rather than allowing them to escalate. Strategies include agreeing to take a break if the conversation becomes heated. During these breaks, each partner can reflect on their feelings without engaging in negative reactions to each other's opinions. It's important to return to the discussion with a mindset of collaboration rather than competition. Using visual aids can also facilitate negotiations. Couples can create charts or lists detailing their preferences and needs, providing a more tangible reference point during discussions. Visually mapping out desires can empower partners to have confrontational discussions more comfortably. It removes some of the weight and subjective nature of verbal negotiations, creating more clarity in communication.

Moreover, involving an unbiased third party, such as a couples' therapist, can also assist in navigating these preferences. Professional guidance can provide couples with new perspectives and tools to address their differences healthily. Sometimes, having an external mediator can alleviate the pressure from the relationship while fostering cooperation between partners.

In cases where one partner's desires significantly overpower the other's, it may be necessary to evaluate the overall dynamics of the relationship. Addressing if there are imbalances in power dynamics or emotional labor is critical. A relationship built on equality allows both partners to feel prioritized and valued, leading to more fruitful negotiations in any aspect, intimacy included.

Finally, remember that negotiation is a continuous process, not a one-time event. Recognizing that preferences may evolve over time encourages an ongoing dialogue that preserves intimacy long-term. Cultivating an attitude of flexibility and openness ensures that partners have the necessary tools to navigate inevitable differences gracefully, thus maintaining the heart of their connection.

Deepening intimacy requires effort and understanding, and the negotiation of preferences is a significant part of that journey. Through open communication, shared goals, and a commitment to respect each other's needs, couples can turn their differences into strengths that enrich their relationships. In this continuous journey, each negotiation becomes an opportunity for growth, deeper understanding, and greater intimacy. With these practical strategies, couples can foster an environment of mutual respect and understanding that allows their relationship to flourish.

Embracing Differences as Strengths

In any committed relationship, differences can often be a source of conflict, misunderstanding, and discontent. However, these variances in personality, preference, and perspective can also serve as a source of strength, providing opportunities for intimacy and growth. Embracing these differences rather than resisting or attempting to change them can deepen the bond between partners, inviting a richer experience that transcends mere physical attraction or emotional connection.

At the heart of intimacy lies understanding—an appreciation for each other's unique qualities. Differences can provide a roadmap for this understanding, offering couples ways to engage with and learn from one another. Many couples can attest to the transformative power of embracing their distinctions. By doing so, they cultivate an intimate environment where vulnerability thrives, and trust deepens.

When we talk about differences, it is essential first to understand the range of ways in which partners might differ. These differences can encompass a wide spectrum, from personality traits to life experiences, communication styles, coping mechanisms, and even cultural backgrounds. Recognizing that each partner brings unique histories and perspectives to the relationship is the first step toward leveraging these distinctions to foster deeper intimacy.

Take, for instance, a couple where one partner is highly extroverted while the other is more introverted. At first glance, this dichotomy may lead to misunderstandings, particularly in social settings. The extroverted partner might feel frustrated by the introvert's need for solitude, while the introvert may feel overwhelmed by the extrovert's desire for social engagement. However, if both partners choose to embrace these differences, the extrovert can learn the value of solitude and reflection, while the introvert can discover the joys of connection and spontaneity. This shared journey allows them to grow individually and together, expanding their emotional horizons and enriching their relationship.

Communication is vital when it comes to embracing differences. It becomes essential for couples to approach their contrasts with curiosity rather than judgment. By actively engaging in open dialogues about their differing preferences and viewpoints, each partner can share their thoughts, feelings, and, importantly, their desires. This fosters an atmosphere of respect and acknowledgment, where both individuals feel safe and valued. Rather than retreating to their corners, they can weave their perspectives together, crafting a shared narrative that honors each other's truth.

One effective strategy to embrace differences involves creating a shared vocabulary around them. By identifying specific differences and labeling them, couples can transform perceptions of their distinctions from potential obstacles to strengths. For example, a couple might openly discuss their differing approaches to conflict resolution—one partner may prefer to address issues head- on, while the other prefers to take time for reflection before discussing matters. By naming these styles, they can create a clearer understanding of each approach, allowing for more effective navigation during disagreements. This conscious articulation of their differences removes the potential for stigmatization and, instead, opens pathways to collaboration and growth.

Practical exercises can also facilitate the embracing of differences. Couples may consider engaging in activities that allow them to step into each other's shoes. For instance, a couple could take turns planning a date based on each other's interests. This exercise not only showcases differences but provides a platform for learning about one another in an enjoyable setting. The extroverted partner might plan a lively gathering with friends, while the introverted partner might opt for a quiet evening spent stargazing or reading together. These experiences enrich shared memories and create a deeper understanding of one another's preferences, demonstrating love and respect for what makes each partner unique.

Additionally, embracing differences promotes a sense of balance within the relationship. Just as yin and yang represent complementary forces, couples can learn to appreciate how their differences harmonize and balance each other. A nurturing environment is created when the assertiveness of one partner is tempered by the thoughtfulness of the other. It allows for a dynamic interplay where both partners contribute their strengths to support one another. This balance creates stability, preventing one partner from overpowering or overshadowing the other.

Moreover, embracing differences can significantly enhance problem-solving skills within the partnership. When a couple approaches challenges with their respective perspectives, they can cultivate a more comprehensive understanding of the situation. The divergent opinions can lead to innovative solutions that neither partner might have considered alone. This collaborative problem-solving not only strengthens the relationship's foundation but also reinforces the idea that together, they can overcome various obstacles.

Furthermore, the beauty of embracing differences extends to the personal development of each partner. As partners encourage each other to explore unfamiliar territory, they embark on a journey of self-discovery. The extroverted partner might gain insights into the importance of introspection, while the introverted partner may develop confidence in social situations. Such growth not only benefits individual partners but also enhances their shared experiences, allowing them to evolve both personally and as a couple.

Conflict management represents another vital arena in which embracing differences can yield positive results. Each partner comes to the relationship equipped with their conflict resolution strategies, reflecting their individual life experiences. By embracing these strategies—whether they be direct, assertive, passive, or avoidant—couples can learn to navigate disputes with compassion and understanding. Instead of viewing a difference in conflict styles as a source of frustration, they can approach it as an opportunity to learn and grow together. Couples can create an environment where the floor is open for each partner to express their feelings safely.

When we reposition differences as strengths, we begin to recognize the potential for deeper emotional intimacy. Embracing what makes individuals distinct opens avenues for exploration and vulnerability, resulting in a connection that transcends the superficial. When individuals express their emotions openly and authentically, they contribute to an intimate atmosphere where both partners feel valued and understood. This profound ability to share one's true self—acknowledging flaws, fears, and hopes—creates a powerful and binding emotional experience.

Moreover, intimacy thrives on the recognition that partners are not perfect, nor do they need to be. They are two individuals, each with their complexities and inconsistencies. By embracing their differences, couples can acknowledge each other's imperfections and choose to love not in spite of them, but because of them. This perspective encourages growth and authenticity in ways that perfectionism never could. It fosters acceptance and kindness, which are essential elements of lasting intimacy.

An illustrative example can be found in couples who have successfully navigated differences during crises or significant life changes. When faced with challenges such as job loss, illness, or the arrival of children, couples who embrace differences can turn to each other, drawing on their unique strengths and perspectives. One partner's ability to stay calm during a storm can complement the other's problem-solving skills, allowing them to approach crises as a united front. As they face challenges together, their bond becomes fortified, illustrating that differences can be a source of strength and resilience.

In relationships where partners fully embrace and celebrate their differences, there emerges a culture of growth and accountability. This supportive environment encourages both partners to seek improvement and transformation, understanding that they are not in it alone. When individuals feel uplifted and appreciated for the qualities they bring to the table, they are more likely to work cohesively toward achieving their shared intimacy goals.

Nevertheless, it is important to recognize that embracing differences is not without its challenges. It requires continuous commitment and open-mindedness. Partners must be willing to confront their biases and assumptions, and practice active listening and empathy while processing their distinctions. This commitment leads to deeper understanding, mutual growth, and ultimately, enhanced intimacy.

In conclusion, the journey of embracing differences as strengths in a relationship fosters a deeper, richer connection between partners. When couples utilize their variations to build emotional intimacy rather than allow them to become barriers, they create a foundation for trust, understanding, and mutual respect. By approaching differences with curiosity and empathy, they honor each other's uniqueness, acknowledge the complexities of their partnership, and foster an environment ripe for growth.

Ultimately, love flourishes when partners choose to celebrate what sets them apart. The beauty of two individuals coming together lies in their ability to inspire one another, transcend limitations, and deepen the connection they share. By embracing differences as strengths, couples embark on a journey of love that is not only enduring but continually evolving.

—— Chapter 10 ——

THE JOURNEY OF INTIMACY

THE JOURNEY OF INTIMACY

The Evolving Nature of Intimacy

Intimacy is a living, breathing element of any relationship, an ever-evolving landscape that experiences transformations as couples grow together. Just as seasons change, so too do the expressions of intimacy that partners share. It is vital for couples to understand that change in intimacy is not only natural but can be immensely beneficial to the longevity and depth of their connection. This chapter seeks to explore how intimacy evolves over time, highlighting the importance of embracing this evolution as a core part of the relationship journey.

From the very beginning of a relationship, intimacy is characterized by its novelty and excitement. The initial stages are often filled with passion, where every touch, kiss, and knowing look ignites a flurry of emotions. During this phase, couples frequently engage in romantic gestures that build strong physical and emotional ties. Enthralled by the discovery of each other, partners connect with an intensity that feels electrifying.

However, as time progresses, the euphoric rush of new love starts to settle into a more profound experience of intimacy. Couples may find that the frequency of passionate encounters may not be as fervent as during the early days. Instead, a different kind of intimacy emerges, one that invites partners to explore deeper vulnerabilities and emotional closeness. Herein lies the beauty of evolving intimacy—what was once a relationship driven by physical attraction now becomes enriched through shared experiences, trust, and understanding.

As relationships mature, the excitement of the initial phase fades, but in its place, couples discover the significance of emotional intimacy. Sharing life's ups and downs, supporting each other through challenges, and building a mutual understanding contribute to a different yet equally fulfilling intimacy. This phase invites couples to engage in meaningful conversations about their dreams, fears, and aspirations.

During this evolution, it's not uncommon for partners to encounter obstacles that can alter the emotional landscape of their intimacy. Issues such as work stress, parenthood, financial strain, or health problems may cast a long shadow over their connection. In such times, it is essential for couples to acknowledge these challenges as part of their shared journey. Navigating these complexities together, when approached with understanding, can deepen intimacy rather than diminish it.

Consider the couple who faced the trials of new parenthood. The arrival of a child can significantly shift the dynamics of intimacy, as physical and emotional resources become stretched. Both partners must learn to navigate their new roles while maintaining their relationship. This can often lead to feelings of isolation, misunderstandings, and a decreased frequency of physical closeness. However, those who approach this transition with open communication and shared goals for maintaining intimacy often find that they can build stronger bonds.

In the face of challenges, it's essential to develop adaptive strategies that allow couples to maintain intimacy in ways that resonate with their current realities. For example, couples may embrace the idea of emotional intimacy through small gestures—an unexpected note, a surprise text, or an evening spent reminiscing about the past. These seemingly minor moments can carry immense significance, rejuvenating the bond that might seem to have diminished.

Moreover, expressingempathy and compassion becomes increasingly vital as intimacy evolves. As partners grow and change individually, recognizing that their needs may not always align is essential. This realization can be an opportunity for couples to explore their differences and allow these variations to enrich their relationship. Rather than letting misunderstandings create barriers, couples can engage in open dialogues about their feelings and desires, adapting their understanding of intimacy in the process.

The rediscovery of intimacy may also manifest in ways couples had not previously experienced. For instance, as relationships age, partners may develop new interests or hobbies, prompting the creation of shared experiences that can reignite emotional and sexual intimacy. This may include exploring new activities together, such as dance classes, cooking experiments, or travel adventures. Engaging in these novel experiences can usher in a rejuvenation of intimacy, allowing couples to reconnect in refreshing and exciting ways.

As partners weather the storms of life together, they often find that the intimacy they once shared has evolved into a deeper understanding of themselves and each other. This can lead to a renewed appreciation for the relationship and a desire to prioritize intimacy actively. Couples may choose to establish regular date nights or seek out moments where they can focus solely on each other, consciously working to uphold their connection.

Over time, the expressions of physical intimacy might also change. Whereas physical touch may have once been frequent and fervent, couples might find that they crave deeper emotional connections rather than purely sexual encounters. This evolution does not signify a decline in intimacy but rather an invitation to explore dimensions of intimacy that were previously unexplored. Partners can forge a bond that deepens as they learn to communicate their needs and desires clearly, enhancing both emotional and physical intimacy in the process.

In exploring the evolving nature of intimacy, it is vital to address the significance of individual growth within a partnership. As partners engage in personal development, whether through education, career advancement, or self-exploration, their individual experiences can positively impact their relationship. A partner who feels fulfilled and nurtured in their individual pursuits often brings a renewed sense of energy and enthusiasm to the relationship. This can create a ripple effect of intimacy, where both partners feel motivated to explore their connection more deeply.

Another aspect of evolving intimacy is the acceptance of change itself. As individuals age, circumstances change, and life presents new challenges, partners are called to adapt. Embracing this notion can be liberating for couples, who can learn that they can still experience intimacy even amid transformation. This adaptability fosters resilience—the capacity to recover from difficulties and strengthen the connection despite life's temporary upheavals.

As the journey of intimacy continues, couples may find that their bodies and preferences evolve as well. Communication about physical intimacy should remain open and honest, allowing for changes in sexual desire or preferences to be discussed without judgment. Partners might need to explore new approaches to physical closeness, actively seeking feedback and engaging in open conversations about their needs. This collaborative effort can lead to heightened satisfaction for both partners, as they navigate the shifting terrain of physical intimacy together.

As intimacy evolves, it becomes essential to celebrate the milestones along the way. Recognizing moments of growth within the relationship—whether it's a wedding anniversary, the birth of a child, or achieving common goals—provides an opportunity for couples to reflect on their journey together. Celebrating these milestones strengthens the bond and serves as a reminder of the love and commitment they share.

Reflecting on the evolving nature of intimacy also requires a willingness to express gratitude for each partner's presence in their life. Even during challenging times when intimacy feels strained, valuing what each partner brings to the relationship keeps the connection alive. A simple acknowledgment of appreciation can work wonders in revitalizing intimacy, reminding both partners of the strengths they share.

In conclusion, the evolving nature of intimacy is a dynamic journey that builds and transforms throughout the course of a relationship. Embracing the shifts that occur over time is paramount for couples seeking to create a lasting emotional and physical connection. As partners honor their relationship's evolution, they give themselves the opportunity to experience deeper intimacy, evolution through resilience, enriching their journey while creating a strong foundation for love and connection.

Celebrating Milestones

Milestones are pivotal moments in the journey of any relationship, marking significant events that serve to deepen the bond between partners. In the context of intimacy, acknowledging these milestones is not just a celebratory act; it serves as a powerful tool for enhancing emotional connection, reinforcing trust, and fostering an environment of love and support. Recognizing and celebrating milestones can transform routine moments into profound expressions of appreciation, growth, and commitment in a partnership.

At various stages in a relationship, couples experience milestones that can range from significant anniversaries to smaller, yet meaningful, events like the completion of a shared project, the birth of a child, or even a personal achievement that holds importance for one partner. Each milestone represents a shared experience that can bring couples closer together by creating opportunities for reflection and appreciation.

For instance, consider a couple celebrating their first anniversary. This occasion is not merely a marker of time passed; it symbolizes the journey they have taken together over the past year. Reflecting on memories made, challenges overcome, and achievements celebrated enables couples to relive their shared history, reinforcing their emotional bond. Such reflections bring to light the areas in which they have grown individually and as a couple, allowing for a deeper understanding of each other's desires and aspirations.

Moreover, the act of celebration itself becomes a meaningful ritual. Whether it is a simple dinner at home, a weekend getaway, or an extravagant party with family and friends, celebrating milestones provides an opportunity for couples to express love and appreciation for one another. During these moments of joy and celebration, partners can openly communicate their feelings, express gratitude, and reaffirm their commitment to one another. This open dialogue fosters a safe space for vulnerability, where partners can share their hopes for the future and any fears or insecurities that may arise as the relationship evolves.

Celebrating milestones is not limited to major anniversaries or events; small, everyday achievements also deserve recognition. For example, completing a difficult project at work together or supporting each other through a challenging period can serve as milestones worth celebrating. By acknowledging these smaller victories, couples deepen their appreciation for one another and cultivate a habit of gratitude. This practice can foster a positive outlook on the relationship, as it emphasizes the importance of collaboration and teamwork.

In addition to enhancing emotional connection, marking milestones can also serve a practical purpose: it creates shared memories that couples can look back on fondly. These shared experiences become touchstones in the relationship—reminders of love, support, and partnership that couples can return to during difficult times. When partners face challenges, they can draw strength from the knowledge that they have weathered storms together in the past, further fortifying their bond.

The importance of recognizing and celebrating these moments is supported by the experiences of many couples. Take, for instance, Laura and James, who have been married for five years.

Every year, they set aside a weekend to celebrate their wedding anniversary by revisiting the venue of their wedding ceremony. Not only does this tradition allow them to reconnect with the emotions of their special day, but it also opens up discussions about their journey since then. They share stories about their first home, the challenges they faced in establishing their careers, and the joys of welcoming their first child. Each anniversary becomes a reflective experience where they can celebrate their love and commitment, and where they can discuss their dreams for the future.

Celebrations don't have to be lavish to be impactful. Emily and Ryan, a couple navigating the ups and downs of raising young children, have created a tradition of celebrating their "mini milestones". For example, after completing a home improvement project together or successfully managing a challenging week with their kids, they take time to acknowledge each other's contributions. They set up a special evening with a favorite meal or movie, during which they discuss what they accomplished and how working together has strengthened their bond. This practice not only enhances intimacy but also promotes a sense of teamwork and shared investment in their family life.

When couples focus on recognizing and celebrating milestones, they cultivate a relationship culture that prioritizes connection. This culture becomes particularly important in long-term relationships, where the novelty can sometimes wear off. By actively celebrating milestones, couples inject excitement and joy back into their partnership.

To truly embrace the significance of milestones, it is essential for partners to communicate openly about what matters to each of them. Each individual may have different interpretations of what a milestone is based on their upbringing, culture, and personal experiences. Understanding these differences can enrich the celebration experience. Therefore, couples should engage in conversations about what milestones are important to them and explore how they can build their own traditions around these moments.

Celebrating milestones can also have a positive impact on individual growth within the relationship. By encouraging one another to pursue personal goals and passions, partners can celebrate achievements that may seem minor but are meaningful for their own development. Recognizing and celebrating a partner's promotion at work, completing a personal project, or achieving a health goal reinforces the idea that both partners contribute uniquely to the relationship.

Moreover, celebrations can act as teaching moments. They can help partners learn about each other's values, priorities, and aspirations. For example, if one partner values public recognition and elaborate celebrations, while the other prefers intimate gatherings, the couple can navigate these differences by finding a compromise that honors both perspectives. This practice not only enhances intimacy but also deepens understanding between partners.

In relationships where milestones are recognized and celebrated, partners often report feeling more connected and supported. The emotional safety fostered by such celebrations allows for deeper expressions of love and vulnerability, which are essential components of intimacy. When partners feel appreciated, they are more likely to express their needs, desires, and fears openly, leading to a stronger emotional connection.

It is important to be mindful of maintaining balance when celebrating milestones. The heart of intimacy lies in the quality of the relationship rather than the quantity or scale of celebrations. Over-emphasizing milestone celebrations can lead to pressure and unrealistic expectations. Instead of focusing on grand measures of celebration, couples should cultivate a mindset that appreciates the moment, however small it may be.

One way to maintain this balance is by ensuring that celebrations feel authentic to both partners. For example, if a couple decides to celebrate the anniversary of their first date, they could plan an evening reminiscent of that day, complete with the same meal they shared. This nostalgia can evoke emotional connections while ensuring that the celebration feels genuine rather than forced.

Furthermore, taking time to express gratitude during these celebrations enhances the experience. Couples can create traditions where they share their appreciation for each other, highlighting specific traits or actions that they value. This practice not only boosts individual self-esteem but also strengthens the bond between partners.

Celebrating milestones becomes a beautiful opportunity for couples to express love, acknowledge growth, and recommit to one another. By embracing both the big and small moments in their journey, partners enhance their emotional connection and deepen their intimacy. In this way, milestones serve not only as markers of time but also as key opportunities for partners to nurture their relationship.

As life progresses and relationships evolve, it is crucial for couples to create an intentional atmosphere of celebration. The act of recognizing milestones—be they small triumphs or significant anniversaries—provides a structure around which intimacy can flourish. Engagement in these practices fosters love, understanding, and support, creating a resilient foundation that couples can rely on as they navigate the complexities of their journey together.

In conclusion, celebrating milestones is an integral part of nurturing intimacy in a relationship. By recognizing both significant and minor achievements, couples can enhance their bond, transform moments of routine into opportunities for reflection and appreciation, and cultivate a tradition of gratitude. Developing a culture of celebration within a relationship reinforces the commitment that partners share, allowing them to grow, connect, and thrive together as they journey through life.

Adapting to Change

In the life of every couple, change is a constant companion, shaping the dynamics of their relationship in profound ways. From the joyful transitions of marriage to the trials of parenthood or career shifts, these life changes demand a level of adaptability that can often be challenging. Yet, it is precisely through navigating these changes together that couples can find an opportunity to deepen their intimacy. Understanding how to maintain closeness—emotionally and physically—amidst the tumultuous waves of change is essential for the sustenance of a healthy relationship.

At the start of a relationship, everything seems straightforward. The initial excitement and passion can create an illusion of permanence. However, as life unfolds, various factors inevitably test the bond: financial stresses, health concerns, changes in careers, the arrival of children, and the ebb and flow of personal ambitions. Each of these transitions can challenge how couples communicate, connect, and support each other. The stakes can feel incredibly high, yet it is in these moments that the principles of adaptability can shine through.

To navigate change effectively, a couple's response to these transitions should not be reactive but proactive. Awareness of the changes occurring is the first step. This awareness cultivates a supportive environment, fostering discussions about how each person is feeling during these transitions. Acknowledging the different emotional responses to change is crucial. For instance, one partner may feel excited about a career shift while the other feels anxious about the unknown. By recognizing these differing emotions, couples can validate each other's feelings and create a safe space to communicate openly.

This communication can be enriched by regular check-ins with one another, allowing time to share thoughts about the changing landscape of their lives. These discussions should occur in a relaxed environment where both partners feel valued and heard. Scheduling a weekly sit-down, perhaps over dinner or during a quiet moment in the evening, can work wonders. During these moments, couples can discuss expectations, fears, and hopes about each of their lives, as well as their relationship. This practice not only reinforces emotional intimacy but also builds a partnership grounded in mutual understanding and shared goals.

Being adaptable also means recognizing when to seek help. Changes can sometimes lead to unresolved conflicts or misunderstandings. Recognizing the need for external support is vital for many couples. Seeking a counselor or therapist can provide couples with tools to navigate their transitions, providing a neutral ground to address and resolve tensions that may arise. It can help couples learn effective communication techniques, establish awareness of harmful patterns, and create strategies for a collective approach to change.

Moreover, adaptability requires couples to be flexible rather than rigid. Life is dynamic, and the ability to pivot in response to unforeseen circumstances is a hallmark of a resilient relationship. Couples should engage in brainstorming sessions when faced with significant changes, collaboratively finding solutions that accommodate both partners' needs and aspirations. For instance, one partner's job may require long hours that disrupt established routines, impacting familial interactions. Open discourse can lead to innovative solutions, such as reorganizing schedules, implementing alone time into weeks, or revisiting and agreeing upon priorities together.

Creativity can also play a key role in maintaining intimacy during times of change. Exploring new activities or experiences together can reignite passion and connection. This could range from learning a new hobby together—like cooking or dancing—to engaging in adventures that challenge comfort zones, such as traveling to new destinations. The thrill of shared experiences can reignite the excitement in the relationship and create cherished memories during transitional times.

Maintaining intimacy also pertains to physical connection, which can sometimes falter during life changes. Stress and fatigue from a new job, for example, can lead to feelings of emotional distance. In recognizing this, partners should prioritize finding time for each other, even if it's just small moments of tenderness—holding hands, loving words, or a warm hug can go a long way. Scheduling intimate moments, no matter how small, reminds couples of their physical bond even amid chaos.

Maintaining a healthy sexual relationship is also paramount during transitions. Life changes can often lead to a decreased libido; however, it's essential to make the effort to keep this aspect of intimacy alive. Couples can experiment with different forms of intimacy beyond penetrative sex, such as sensual massages, cuddling, or simply enjoying shared moments as they lie close to one another. By redefining the parameters of physical connection and allowing intimacy to unfold in various forms, couples can foster a deeper level of emotional intimacy.

Rituals are another way to anchor a couple's intimacy, providing stability amid change. Rituals—whether large or small—create predictability in a relationship, allowing couples to have shared experiences that connect them together. This could involve a simple routine of having coffee together every morning before starting daily activities or a dedicated date night each week. These rituals create moments of connection, comfort, and reliability—critical components in fostering intimacy.

As life unfolds, seasoned couples may find ways to redefine their goals and shared visions. Major life shifts can offering an opportunity to revisit dreams and desires that may have been left behind. Perhaps a partner has long-held aspirations of starting a business or pursuing a specific career path. Encouraging and supporting each other in the pursuit of individual goals can deepen connection, aligning both partners toward shared growth. This mutual encouragement allows couples not only to adapt to change but thrive as individuals and as a team.

Learning how to adapt is an ongoing process; it requires patience and understanding, both of which are fundamental in a relationship. Every couple will face periods of adjustment, but embracing these times can strengthen the bond over time.

Remaining patient when conflicts arise, understanding that periods of distance can occur, all add layers of resilience to the partnership.

Emotional intelligence can also significantly enhance adaptability in a relationship. Partners should strive to cultivate a high degree of emotional awareness, not only of one's own needs but also of those of the partner. Recognizing shifts in emotional states—whether due to work stress, family dynamics, or personal growth—allows couples to address issues quickly before they fester. This understanding can help couples to adjust their responses, ultimately supporting each other through transitions more effectively.

Amid changes, personal growth is inevitable, and how couples approach this growth together can either strengthen their bond or create distance. It's essential to openly discuss aspirations and feelings about changes that are unfolding and how they align with each partner's growth trajectory. Emphasizing empathy and encouragement during these discussions can help create a shared narrative of finding comfort in each other's journeys.

Celebrating successes together is also vital in the face of change. Acknowledging and celebrating milestones—no matter how small—helps to reinforce the connection and provides motivation for both partners. Whether it's a new job, a project completion, or overcoming a challenge, recognition of these achievements can fuel positivity and closeness.

Seasonal changes, too, can impact intimacy and connection. Just as nature cycles through seasons, relationships experience phases of growth and dormancy. Not every phase will yield flourishing fruit, but understanding and respecting these cycles can assist in navigating transitions. During quieter seasons, partnersmight need to lay the groundwork for deeper understanding and connection, reestablishing their bond for a fruitful future phase.

Ultimately, adaptability in relationships is not just about managing change; it's about fostering a partnership based on the principles of support, empathy, and love. Couples that learn the art of adaptability emerge not only as survivors of life's challenges but as stronger, more connected partners. Every transition presents a choice: to resist change and cling to the past or to embrace it, releasing the comfort of familiarity for the thrill of new beginnings.

In conclusion, the journey of intimacy is richly textured and deeply influenced by the inevitability of change. By recognizing the necessity of adaptability, couples can harness life's transitions as opportunities for growth, intimacy, and connection. Through open communication, shared experiences, and mutual support, couples can navigate the turbulent waters of life together, emerging stronger and more united than ever.

Chapter 11

CREATING YOUR INTIMACY BLUEPRINT

CREATING YOUR INTIMACY BLUEPRINT

Assessing Your Relationship

In the intricate tapestry of relationships, intimacy serves as one of the most vital threads. However, assessing where we stand on this continuum of closeness can often feel daunting. It requires a level of honesty and vulnerability that many couples find challenging. Yet, a self-assessment of your relationship's intimacy levels is crucial for growth and a deeper connection.

This chapter aims to guide you through a structured evaluation of your current intimacy levels, highlighting strengths and identifying possible areas for growth. Intimacy is not a static concept; it ebbs and flows based on numerous factors, including life experiences, communication styles, and external stressors. At times, you may feel incredibly connected to your partner, while at other times, you might notice a growing distance. A regular self-assessment helps counter this ebb and flow, allowing you to actively cultivate the intimacy you desire. As you embark on this self-assessment, it's essential to create a space for open and honest dialogue. Encourage your partner to engage in this process with you; intimacy is a shared journey.

The following sections will guide you in evaluating emotional, physical, and sexual intimacy, enabling you to gain a comprehensive understanding of your relationship's landscape.

Emotional Intimacy

Emotional intimacy is the foundation of close relationships. It involves fostering a safe environment where both partners feel comfortable sharing their innermost thoughts, fears, and dreams. Start your assessment here, as emotional connection often influences other types of intimacy.

Reflect on Emotional Availability:

Begin by evaluating your emotional availability and that of your partner. Emotional availability means being present and engaging with your partner on a deeper level. Consider questions such as:

- Do you feel comfortable expressing your feelings and vulnerabilities?
- Are you able to listen to your partner without judgment?
- How often do you engage in conversations about your emotional well-being?

Discuss these questions with your partner. One way to make this dialogue more organic is to frame it as a casual conversation rather than a formal interview. By doing so, you encourage a free flow of thoughts and foster a more relaxed environment.

Sharing Vulnerabilities:

Another aspect of emotional intimacy is the ability to share vulnerabilities. These can include fears, insecurities, and past experiences that have shaped who you are. Ask yourselves:

- Do you openly share your vulnerabilities with each other?
- How does your partner respond when you share something personal?
- Do you feel supported when discussing difficult subjects?

Vulnerability can be terrifying, but it's essential for growth. When one partner shares openly, it creates a ripple effect, encouraging the other to reciprocate. Make it a point to share one vulnerability each week, allowing this practice to become a regular component of your emotional interaction.

Identifying Communication Styles:

Communication is critical in emotional intimacy. Every individual has a unique communication style that can affect how effectively they connect with their partner. Reflect on:

- How do you communicate your emotions?
- Are your styles compatible, or do they clash?
- Do misunderstandings frequently lead to conflict, or are you able to navigate challenges with effective communication?

Understanding each other's communication styles opens a pathway to addressing emotional distance. If difficulties arise, consider seeking the support of a communication expert or therapist who can provide tailored strategies.

Physical Intimacy

Physical intimacy encompasses the non-sexual aspects of closeness—affectionate touch, hugs, and holding hands, which are vital for maintaining emotional bonds. It's essential for couples to assess whether they are on the same page regarding physical intimacy.

Evaluate Frequency and Type of Touch:

Begin by discussing the frequency and nature of physical touch in your relationship:

- How often do you engage in physical affection outside of sexual interactions?
- Are there specific types of touch that you both enjoy?
- Do you feel comfortable expressing your need for physical contact?

Touch can range from simple gestures to more intimate forms. Explore what feels comfortable to both of you and make a conscious effort to incorporate more affection into your daily interactions.

Emphasize activities like holding hands while walking or cuddling during a movie as foundational elements of physical intimacy.

Creating Safe Spaces for Touch:

It's pivotal to create safe spaces where both partners feel encouraged to explore physical intimacy comfortably. Ask yourselves:

- Are there areas in your home that foster closeness?
- Do you have regular rituals that promote intimacy, such as date nights or evening walks?
- How do you communicate your comfort levels regarding physical closeness?

Invest time in creating intentional moments for physical connection. Perhaps designate a day of the week for intimacy-building activities, be it a massage exchange or simply spending quiet time together in touch.

Discussing Boundaries and Preferences:

Every individual has unique preferences regarding physical intimacy. Take time to discuss and establish boundaries that work for both partners:

- Are there areas where one partner feels uncomfortable?
- How can you navigate these preferences without creating tension or resentment?
- Do you frequently check in with each other about your comfort levels?

By discussing boundaries openly, you create space for understanding and respect, which fosters a deeper bond between you.

Sexual Intimacy

Sexual intimacy is often considered the climax of connection, but it can also be the most challenging to assess due to personal insecurities and societal pressures. However, understanding your sexual intimacy levels is crucial for holistic relationship wellness.

Evaluate Sexual Satisfaction:

Begin by reflecting on sexual satisfaction:

- How satisfied are you with your sex life?
- Are there aspects that either of you wishes to enhance or change?
- Do you feel comfortable openly discussing your sexual desires?

Establishing a climate where both partners feel safe discussing sexual satisfaction can significantly impact the quality of your intimacy. Consider scheduling regular "intimacy check-ins" to openly discuss desires, preferences, and any adjustments you wish to make.

Understanding Changes in Sexual Desire:

Sexual desire often fluctuates throughout a relationship, influenced by various factors like stress or life transitions. Reflect on:

- Have you noticed any changes in your sexual desire?
- How do you both respond to fluctuations in libido?
- Are there external factors that play a role in your sexual intimacy, such as parenting or work stress?

Understanding the ebb and flow of sexual desire aids in mitigating disappointment or resentment. Acknowledging that fluctuations are normal allows you to remain compassionate and patient with each other.

Exploring New Experiences:

Exploration can rejuvenate sexual intimacy. Discuss:

- Have you found ways to explore new experiences in your sexual life?

- Are you both comfortable introducing new elements, such as different locations or activities?
- How do you navigate the introduction of novelty into your intimacy?

Introduce new experiences with open dialogue, emphasizing that exploring does not imply dissatisfaction with your current sexual life. Being open to trying new things creates a shared sense of adventure and can reignite passion.

Identifying Strengths

Having delved into emotional, physical, and sexual intimacy, it's essential to identify the strengths that exist in your relationship. Recognizing these strengths offers a foundation upon which you can build further intimacy.

Celebrate Successful Communication:

As you discuss your experiences in the intimacy assessment, highlight moments of successful communication. Recognize:

- Instances when you navigated challenges effectively together.
- How you've overcome misunderstandings and emerged stronger.
- The positive impact of vulnerability and openness on your relationship.

Celebrating these moments fosters a sense of partnership and reinforces the notion that you can overcome challenges together.

Acknowledge Moments of Closeness:

Reflect on specific instances of closeness and connection:

- When do you feel most connected to your partner?
- Are there rituals or activities that enhance feelings of intimacy?

Acknowledging the moments where intimacy flourishes can help maintain and replicate those experiences.

Recognize Shared Resilience:

Strength often manifests in resilience. Consider:

- How have you navigated difficult times together?
- What has helped your relationship stand strong during challenges?

Recognizing resilience hones your ability to face future challenges with confidence, knowing you have weathered storms before, and emerged closer for it.

Identifying Areas for Growth

While recognizing strengths is vital, it's equally essential to identify areas where growth may be necessary. By openly discussing these areas, couples can foster deeper intimacy.

Spotting Communication Gaps:

If communication has been a challenge, prompt an honest dialogue:

- Are there recurring topics that evoke tension?
- How might you alter your communication styles for increased harmony?

Seeking understanding and compromise can help eliminate misunderstandings.

Addressing Hesitance in Vulnerability:

If vulnerability feels challenging, explore why that might be:

- Are there fears rooted in past experiences?
- How can you create a safe space to nurture vulnerability?

Dedicate time to practicing sharing vulnerabilities with each other, reinforcing that vulnerability is a strength.

Navigating Sexual Compatibility:

Evaluate how sexual compatibility plays a role:- Are there discrepancies in sexual desire or preferences?- How can you work together to bridge these gaps?Regular dialogue around sexual compatibility can cultivate a supportive atmosphere for exploration and growth.Moving Forward TogetherThis self-assessment is not merely an evaluation; it's a commitment to ongoing growth and understanding within your relationship. Regular check-ins can enable you and your partner to adapt, nurture, and explore intimacy in new ways.

Creating an Intimacy Action Plan:

Consider developing a plan based on your insights:- What steps can you both take to enhance intimacy in emotional, physical, and sexual realms?- Are there specific actions you can commit to regularly to nurture closeness?By collectively drafting an intimacy plan, you create accountability and reinforce the importance of nurturing your bond.

Celebrating Progress:

As you embark on this journey of intimacy enhancement, celebrate your progress regularly. Acknowledge milestones, no matter how small, as they reinforceyour commitment to one another.

Embracing Change:

Finally, recognize that your relationship will continually evolve. What works today may need adjustments tomorrow. Embrace this dynamic nature, understanding that the journey towards deeper intimacy is ongoing and filled with opportunities for connection.In summary, assessing your relationship's intimacy levels is a crucial step towards fostering a deeper connection with your partner. By evaluating emotional, physical, and sexual intimacy, recognizing strengths, and identifying areas for growth, you set a solid foundation for ongoing intimacy development. Communicate openly, hold each other accountable, and cultivate a strong partnership that thrives in closeness and connection. Love, after all, is a journey, and every step brings you both closer together.

Setting Goals for Intimacy

Setting goals for intimacy is a crucial step in enhancing the connection between partners. Just as individuals create personal goals in various aspects of their lives, couples should also take the time to set clear and achievable goals for their intimate relationship. This shared endeavor not only fosters alignment in desires and expectations but also cultivates a deeper understanding of one another's needs and aspirations. Through thoughtful discussions and purposeful exercises, couples can create a roadmap to intimacy that nurtures connection, vulnerability, and mutual support.

As you embark on this journey to enhance intimacy, consider the following steps and exercises designed to guide your conversations and reflections.

Understanding the Importance of Intimacy Goals

Before diving into the specific exercises, it's essential to comprehend why setting intimacy goals matters. Goals give direction and purpose to your relationship. They transform vague notions of intimacy into concrete actions, helping both partners feel more engaged and invested in nurturing their bond. Furthermore, setting goals can lead to multiple benefits, including:

1. Clarity and Focus: Having clearly defined goals allows both partners to understand each other's expectations, desires, and boundaries, thus reducing ambiguity in the relationship.

2. Enhanced Communication: Discussing intimacy goals fosters open communication. Partners learn to articulate their

needs, fears, and hopes, building a foundation of trust and transparency.

3. Increased Engagement: Working towards a common goal encourages teamwork. Both partners become active participants in their relationship's growth, strengthening their bond.

4. Motivation for Change: Goals can serve as a motivating factor to make necessary changes in the relationship. They prompt partners to take actionable steps towards the intimacy they desire.

5. Celebrating Progress: Setting goals allows couples to measure progress along the way. Celebrating small achievements fosters positive reinforcement and encourages ongoing efforts.

Exercise 1: Reflecting on Current Intimacy

The first step in setting intimacy goals is to assess your current level of intimacy. Take a moment to reflect individually and then share your thoughts with each other. This reflection will provide a baseline for what you wish to achieve.

1. Individual Reflection: Spend a few quiet moments writing down your thoughts on the following prompts:
   - What does intimacy mean to me?
   - How satisfied am I with our current level of intimacy (on a scale of 1-10)?
   - What aspects of intimacy do I feel we are strong in? (e.g., emotional, physical, intellectual, spiritual)
   - What areas of intimacy do I feel need improvement?
   - When do I feel most connected to my partner?

2. Sharing Insights: After reflecting, sit down together and share your thoughts. Discuss:

- What were your surprising insights?
- Did you discover any common themes in your reflections?
- How do you feel about the level of intimacy in your relationship?
- What would you like to see change?

Exercise 2: Visioning Your Intimacy

Once you understand your current intimacy, the next step is to envision what you would like your intimacy to look like in the future. This exercise opens the door to creative thinking and dreaming together.

1. Create a Shared Vision Board: Gather materials such as magazines, scissors, glue, and a poster board.
   - Each partner should cut out images, quotes, or phrases that signify what intimacy looks like for them. Examples could include happy couples, romantic settings, or words expressing connection, trust, and love.
   - Together, arrange the visuals on the poster board, discussing the meaning behind each item you select. This visual representation will serve as a daily reminder of your goals.

2. Verbalize Your Vision: After creating your vision board, take turns verbalizing your ideal future regarding intimacy. Explain:
   - What does an intimate relationship feel like to you?
   - How do you envision spending quality time together?
   - What rituals do you see becoming part of your intimate life?
   - How is your dream realized in daily interactions?

Exercise 3: Defining Specific Intimacy Goals

With a clearer understanding of your current intimacy and a shared vision for the future, it's time to set specific, measurable goals. Good goals should be SMART—Specific, Measurable, Achievable, Relevant, and Time-bound.

1. Brainstorm Goals: Set aside uninterrupted time to brainstorm potential intimacy goals. Think about categories like emotional intimacy, physical intimacy, communication, and shared experiences. Example goals might include:
   - Emotional: Schedule a weekly 'couples check-in' to discuss feelings and needs.
   - Physical: Aim for physical affection at least once daily, even if it's just holding hands or hugs.
   - Communication: Practice active listening for 10 minutes daily without distractions.
   - Experiences: Plan a monthly date night to explore new activities together.

2. Select Your Goals: Review your brainstormed list, then work together to prioritize and select the goals that resonate most with both partners. Discuss:
   - Why do each of us find these goals meaningful?
   - Are any of the goals more essential for the short term than others?
   - How will we hold each other accountable for these goals?

Exercise 4: Establishing a Timeline

Establishing a timeline for your goals is crucial to achieving them. This ensures you remain on track and can focus your efforts. Consider the following:

1. Short-term vs. Long-term Goals: Distinguish between goals to achieve within a month, six months, and even a year. Short-term goals might focus on establishing new routines, whereas long-term goals could delve into deeper vulnerability or increased physical intimacy.

2. Create a Schedule: Using a calendar or planner, schedule regular check-ins where you'll assess your progress towards your intimacy goals. Determine:
   - How often will you check in? Weekly, bi-weekly, or monthly?

— What format will these check-ins take? Will they be casual conversations or structured meetings?

Exercise 5: Accountability Partners

Holding each other accountable for your intimacy goals can significantly boost your chances of success. Cultivating this mutual support gives both partners a sense of responsibility.

1. Choose Accountability Practices: Discuss how you want to support each other. Potential practices might include:
   — Sending each other reminders about your goals.
   — Sharing daily or weekly reflections on your progress.
   — Offering compliments or celebrating small victories.

2. Commit to Regular Check-ins: Ensure that during your scheduled meetings, you discuss what you've accomplished, any challenges you faced, and areas needing more work. Foster an environment free of judgment, where both partners can feel safe discussing their experiences.

Exercise 6: Open Communication and Feedback

Healthy communication is paramount for goal-setting to lead to genuine change. Being open and willing to provide feedback helps partners recalibrate their goals as they grow.

1. Creating an Open Feedback Culture: Establish norms where both partners can express their feelings and feedback constructively. Consider discussing:
   — How do we feel about our progress?
   — Are there any boundaries that need revisiting?
   — What has worked well, and what needs adjustment?

2. Encourage Constructive Criticism: Approach feedback with sensitivity. Use "I" statements to express feelings without blaming. For example, instead of saying, "You never pay attention," try, "I feel neglected when we don't have our dedicated check-in time."

Celebrating Your Progress

As you work towards your intimacy goals, it's vital to celebrate your achievements, both big and small. Celebrating progress reinforces positive behavior and encourages continued growth together.

1. Establish a Reward System: Create fun rewards to recognize your achievements. For instance, after completing a month of consistent communication, plan a special date or weekend getaway.

2. Reflect On What You've Learned: After discussing achievements, take time to reflect on lessons learned along the journey. Engage in conversations about:
    – How have our goals shaped our intimacy?
    – What have we learned about ourselves and each other?
    – Are there new goals that have emerged from this process?

Setting intimacy goals is an ongoing journey. It requires patience, commitment, and a willingness to navigate vulnerabilities and strengths together. By using exercises and prompts to foster thoughtful discussions, couples can create a dynamic intimacy blueprint that evolves alongside their relationship.

As this journey unfolds, remember that it's okay to adjust your goals as needed. Life situations may change, and what worked before might require reevaluation. Embrace adaptability and flexibility as core principles in your commitment to enhancing intimacy.

The outcomes of this process may lead to deeper connections, renewed passion, and an enriched understanding of one another. Ultimately, the dedication to setting and achieving intimacy goals reflects a couple's willingness to invest time and energy into creating a fulfilling, loving partnership.

Action Plan for Success

As couples embark on the journey of enhancing their intimacy, it becomes essential to have a structured plan in place. An action plan serves not just as a roadmap but as a motivating force that helps couples visualize their goals and break them down into manageable steps. This section will guide you through crafting an actionable intimacy plan tailored specifically to your relationship. We will explore practical steps for implementing your intimacy goals, with a focus on accountability and continuous growth.

To begin, the first step is to reflect deeply on what intimacy means for both partners individually. Take time to understand your own needs and desires. This self-awareness lays the groundwork for open discussions, allowing you to articulate what you hope to achieve together. Consider answering the following questions:

1. What does emotional intimacy look like for you?
2. How do you define physical intimacy?
3. What activities or experiences make you feel the closest to your partner?
4. Are there past experiences that have shaped your views on intimacy?

Setting the stage for these conversations requires creating a safe and open environment. Choose a comfortable setting where both partners can express themselves freely without interruptions. You can start your conversation with a gentle prompt like, "I'd love to talk about how we can strengthen our bond. What areas do you feel we can improve on?" This invites dialogue while showing your partner that you genuinely wish to understand their perspective.

Once you've had this initial discussion, it's crucial to formulate your intimacy goals collaboratively. Each partner should come prepared with at least three goals related to emotional and physical intimacy. Write them down, and share them with each other. While discussing these goals, aim for specificity. Instead of a vague goal like "spend more time together," go deeper with something like "we will dedicate one evening a week for a date night where we can connect without distractions."

After identifying your intimacy goals, categorize them into short- term and long-term objectives. Short-term goals can be achievable within a few weeks to a couple of months, while long-term goals might span several months to years. Here's how you can structure them:

Short-Term Goals:

- Schedule regular heart-to-heart talks every Sunday evening to check in on each other's emotional state.
- Experiment with different forms of physical touch, such as cuddling or holding hands, during shared activities.
- Attend a couple's workshop or read a book about intimacy together.

Long-Term Goals:

- Establish an annual getaway focused on reconnecting emotionally and physically away from everyday responsibilities.
- Create a shared passion project that deepens your bond, like volunteering together or taking a class.
- Build a regular tradition to celebrate milestones that acknowledge your journey as a couple, be it anniversaries, achievements, or personal growth.

With your goals defined, the next step is developing actionable steps for each goal. This can be done by breaking them down into smaller, manageable tasks. For each goal, ask:

- What specific steps do we need to take to achieve this?
- Who will be responsible for each task?
- What resources or tools might we need?

As an example, let's take the goal of scheduling a weekly date night. The actionable steps might include:

- Taking turns planning the date each week: Partner A plans week one, Partner B plans week two.
- Creating a shared calendar to block out time for the date night.
- Brainstorming a list of activities ahead of time to avoid decision fatigue.

The accountability factor is crucial for ensuring you and your partner stay on track with your action plan. Implement strategies that strengthen your commitment to each other's goals. Here are a few techniques:

1. Regular Check-Ins:Set aside time every few weeks for a relationship check-in where both of you discuss your progress toward intimacy goals. This isn't just a time to note any struggles but also an opportunity to celebrate victories.

2. Use Visual Reminders: Create a visual representation of your goals and progress, such as a vision board or a shared journal, to keep your objectives front of mind. Incorporate motivational quotes or images that inspire you both.

3. Accountability Partners: Beyond just each other, consider enlisting trusted friends or mentors who can offer support and encouragement. Sharing your goals with them adds an extra layer of commitment.

4. Reward System: Establish a reward system for achieving specific targets. For instance, once a short-term goal is met, take a day trip together or enjoy a favorite meal out. This celebrates your hard work and reinforces positive behavior.

5. Be Flexible and Adapt:Life can be unpredictable. If a certain strategy or goal seems to create stress rather than connection, adjust it. Investigate what is working and what isn't, and remain open to changing the plan as your relationship evolves.

Emphasizing the importance of emotional and physical safety is paramount. Couples should be transparent and vulnerable in discussing their feelings about intimacy. Ground rules about sharing feelings should be established early in this process to avoid misunderstandings. Consider implementing practices like:

- Active Listening: Ensuring that each partner feels heard while discussing their needs. This means putting aside judgments and responses until the speaker has finished expressing their thoughts.

- Nonviolent Communication: This technique can help articulate needs without placing blame. Structure statements by expressing your feelings, needs, and requests clearly. For instance, "I feel neglected when we don't have time together, and I need more quality time. Could we set aside three evenings this month?" Communication tools can enhance the experience of implementing your intimacy action plan. Exploring modalities such as:

- Journaling: This encourages expressing emotions and thoughts privately first, which can then be shared during check-ins.

- Apps or Online Resources: Leverage technology with apps aimed at couples that offer reminders, tips, or daily questions that promote intimacy.

After discussing practical implementation steps, it's vital to evaluate progress regularly. Encourage one another to keep a journal documenting thoughts and feelings surrounding intimacy. Reflect on:

- What strategies have brought you closer?
- Are there areas needing improvements or changes?
- What unexpected joys did you discover along your intimacy journey?

Finally, it's important to remember that intimacy is a journey, not a destination. The action plan for enhancing intimacy within your relationship is dynamic and will evolve over time. Be patient with yourselves, respect each other's boundaries, and celebrate growth.

As you move forward with your intimacy action plan, bear in mind that the ultimate goal is not merely to achieve a checklist of objectives but to foster a loving and deeply connected relationship that withstands the tests of time. The commitment to nurturing intimacy is a continual cycle of growth, learning, and adapting together.

In conclusion, taking responsible and committed action toward enhancing intimacy leads to the creation of a fulfilling relationship that reflects your shared values and desires. By being intentional and dedicated to the process—as well as open to learning and adapting—you will pave the way for a profound sense of closeness that enriches your marriage, fortifying the bond you share in body and soul.

——— Chapter 12 ———

CONCLUSION

Until Next Time, Fellow Explorers

Wow! Can you believe we've reached the end of this vibrant journey together? It feels like just yesterday we were setting sail into uncharted waters, and now here we are, navigating through the waves of thoughts and insights gained along the way. First and foremost, thank you! Your presence in this adventure has made it an unforgettable experience, and your time is truly appreciated.

I hope these pages have stirred something within you. Each story, fact, and reflection is a piece of a larger puzzle that I truly hope has sparked your curiosity and engaged your mind. If you've found even a glimmer of inspiration, then my mission is accomplished. I want you to carry these reflections into your life, to challenge the mundane, to provoke thought, and to incite action. Let this book be a launching pad for your own explorations and discoveries.

Remember, this isn't just a one-time encounter; it's the beginning of an ongoing dialogue. Dig deeper, unleash those questions, and don't let the fire of curiosity fizzle out! Go out there, share your dreams, and connect with the world around you. There's a vast tapestry of stories waiting for your unique contribution, and I can't wait to hear how you make your mark.

If you've enjoyed this journey even half as much as I have, I encourage you to reach out! I'd love to hear your thoughts, experiences, and reflections. So drop me a line, connect with me on social media, or simply spread the word. Your engagement is invaluable and can inspire countless others to embark on their own journeys of exploration.

In this fast-paced world where we tend to rush from one thing to the next, I hope this book serves as a gentle reminder: take the time to slow down, reflect, and let yourself be inspired. Don't forget to savor the moments, nurture the thoughts spurred by these stories, and perhaps even create your own! Together, we can continue this beautiful dialogue that transcends pages and screens.

So, my fellow explorers, as we turn the last page of this book, remember that the adventure doesn't end here. It's just the beginning! Keep dreaming, keep exploring, and always remain curious. Let's stay connected; I'll be here, cheering you on every step of the way.

With zest and gratitude
Prof. Michael T. Adenitire